If God Be For Us

IF GOD BE FOR US

SERMONS ON THE GIFTS OF THE GOSPEL

by

ROBERT E. LUCCOCK

HARPER & BROTHERS
NEW YORK

IF GOD BE FOR US

FIRST EDITION

G-D

Library of Congress catalog card number: 54-8967

To Barbara and to Susan and Nancy

In hope that nothing may ever separate them from the love of God in Jesus Christ

Acknowledgments

The author wishes to express his appreciation to the following authors, agents, and publishers for permission to quote from their copyrighted works:

Anderson House for the lines from *The Eve of St. Mark* and *Lost in the Stars* by Maxwell Anderson. *Lost in the Stars* permission also of William Sloane Associates, Inc.

The Bobbs-Merrill Company, Inc. for "Kings and Stars" from *Sonata and Other Poems* by John Erskine.

Harcourt, Brace and Company, Inc. for "The Hollow Men," "The Cocktail Party," and "The Journey of the Magi," from *The Complete Poems and Plays* of T. S. Eliot.

Jonathan Cape, Ltd. for "A Prayer for the Healing of the Wounds of Christ" from *The Collected Poems of Laurence Housman;* and "The Hound of Heaven" from *The Selected Poems* by Francis Thompson. The lines from "The Hound of Heaven" are reprinted also with the permission of the Executors of the Estate of Francis Thompson.

Dodd, Mead & Company, Inc. for "The House of Christmas" from *Collected Poems of G. K. Chesterton;* and for "Safety" from *Collected Poems of Ruppert Brooke.*

Harper & Brothers for "Thanksgiving" from *The Healing of the Waters* by Amos Wilder.

Henry Holt and Company, Inc. for "The Road Not Taken" from *Mountain Interval* by Robert Frost.

Lilith Lorraine for "When Planes Outsoar the Spirit" from *Let the Patterns Break* by Lilith Lorraine.

The Macmillan Company for "The Coming of Christ" by John Masefield; and "The Widow in the Bye Street" and "The Everlasting Mercy" from *The Poems of John Masefield.*

Virgil Markham for "The Consecration of the Common Way" by Edwin Markham.

Random House, Inc. for *The Age of Anxiety* by W. H. Auden.

Charles Scribner's Sons for "With You a Part of Me" from *Poems* by George Santayana.

Contents

Foreword

"The fruit of the Spirit is love, joy, peace, patience, kindness, goodness, faithfulness, gentleness, self-control. . . ." Each age has made its own restatement of Paul's classic faith. So must it ever be. The main burden of the preacher's message, however variously he may broadcast it, can be no other than the proclamation of the gifts with which the good news of God in Christ has endowed men. If God is for us it means release from anxiety, healing for loneliness, assurance that life is not lost in any kind of frustration. Because God is our friend it means release from life's prisons, redemption of suffering, the fellowship of the Church in our conflict with evil. Since we who were once far off have been brought near it means a new authority to trust, a new discipline of worship, a new hope beyond death. I have tried in these pages to present these central endowments of the Christian faith in fresh, vivid, compelling ways, in the framework of today's world. People are hungry to know what the gospel has to give them for their greatest needs. They need further to understand what their greatest needs are.

I have little patience with anyone who would *use* the gospel as a means of getting something else, whether it be peace of mind, or release from anxiety, or whatever else is lacking at the moment. The gospel is that while we were yet sinners Christ died for us, that we might be delivered from the power of sin and death, and brought into eternal life with God. That is the gospel. No more is needed. In the face of that fact, these other considerations pale as the stars before the rising sun. As we confront people with the gospel it must ever be in terms of the difference which this good news can make to them. "If God be for us . . . then all these gifts are yours to claim."

Conceived and delivered first as sermons, these chapters have all been rewritten as the ruling theme of the book was threaded through them. They were not all preached as part of one series, but representing the effort of sustained preaching to declare the gifts of the gospel the book does have an inner unity. Through much of the book the manner of direct address and many of the pulpit colloquialisms have been retained. Not the most favorable literary style, since preaching loses most of its power in transfer to print anyway, we keep what we can of its original form that it may better speak to the heart. Introducing the sermons are texts from the Gospels and from Paul's epistles. The sermons are not intended as expositions of these verses, but the Scripture passages keep the preaching anchored in the Christian soil.

I am in great spiritual debt to the people of the Church of the Redeemer in New Haven, Connecticut, who received these words with kind and generous hearts, giving back to their minister more than he gave them.

New Haven, Connecticut — Robert E. Luccock
March 15, 1954

If God Be For Us

1

The Inescapable Presence of God

God's Inescapable Presence

> Lo, I am with you always, to the close of the age.
> —Matthew 28:20
>
> For I am sure that . . . nothing in all creation will be able to separate us from the love of God in Jesus Christ our Lord.—Romans 8:39

Two of the loftiest passages of Scripture in the whole Bible have one thing in common: they drive deeply into our minds a fundamental truth in the Christian gospel: the inescapable presence of God. Listen to the writer of the 139th Psalm:

> Whither shall I go from thy Spirit?
> Or whither shall I flee from thy presence?
> If I ascend to heaven, thou art there!
> If I make my bed in Sheol, thou art there!
> If I take the wings of the morning
> and dwell in the uttermost parts of the sea,
> even there shall thy hand lead me,
> and thy right hand shall hold me.

Listen to Paul writing to the Romans:

> If God is for us, who is against us? . . . For I am sure that neither death, nor life, nor angels, nor principalities, nor things present, nor things to come, nor powers, nor height, nor depth, nor anything else in all creation will be able to separate us from the love of God in Jesus Christ our Lord.

In these sermons we shall be concerned with the endowments which Christian faith bestows upon us. We begin with that which underlies all the others: that presence of God from which we cannot run away. The Bible is altogether persuaded that try as you will, go where you may, you can never escape from God.

Moreover, this is no academic proposition of theology. It makes a decided difference to the way you handle life whether you believe that you can flee from God's presence, or whether with the psalmist you believe that if you "take the wings of the morning and dwell in the uttermost parts of the sea," even there shall God's hand lead you. It makes a great difference to what you make out of life whether you believe that you can fall or drift out of God's care, or whether you can say with Paul, "I am sure that nothing in all creation can separate us from the love of God."

"But," someone is asking, "who would want to escape from God? The question is irrelevant." Let's not be too sure about that. Men and women do try to flee from God, for His presence often makes us exceedingly uncomfortable. There are times when all of us would like nothing better than to escape the troublesome presence of God when He makes us ashamed of ourselves and disturbs the easy devices and desires of our own hearts. Furthermore, life holds no more terrible experience than to feel that we have been abandoned by God. Not that we want to escape from Him, but that He has forsaken us; this is what tears some people all to pieces, the consequence of having lost the faith of the 139th Psalm. And at the last how many there are who approach life's end with the conviction that whatever has been their relationship to God in this life, death is the final escape from God: seeing nothing ahead but dissolution for the body and oblivion for the soul. You see, it does make a difference, our persuasion as to His presence.

One of the best-loved poems of Robert Frost is called "The Road Not Taken."[1]

> Two roads diverged in a yellow wood,
> And sorry I could not travel both
> And be one traveller, long I stood
> And looked down one as far as I could
> To where it bent in the undergrowth;
>
> Then took the other, . . .
>
> I shall be telling this with a sigh
> Somewhere ages and ages hence:
> Two roads diverged in a wood and I—
> I took the one less travelled by,
> And that has made all the difference.

Is this an allegory pointing to some of the forks in life's road past which we all must journey? What difference does it make which road we choose to follow?

1. One fork where the ways of life divide is the point at which all of us must decide who will be the Master of our lives, the Captain of our souls. That decision will be determined by whether we believe that all life is held in God's hands, whether we believe that though we journey from here to Timbuktu we are still in God's keeping, His controlling touch still upon all the consequences of our behavior, or whether we believe that we can take life out of God's hands and make the consequences whatever we want. You do not have to look far to see that people often believe they can escape from God by ignoring Him, by seizing the reins and driving off in pursuit of their own desires. And God lets us go, to the end of the tether; sometimes the tether stretches to incredible lengths. But it is never long enough to avoid our being overtaken by Him, for He makes His presence felt first in the stir-

rings of conscience, and where conscience is either ignored or dead we are reminded by His judgment. Paul tried to get away but God overtook him on the Damascus Road.

In one of the great poems of modern literature Francis Thompson describes the inescapable pursuit of God, using the figure of the Hound of Heaven. The poet wrote out of his own experience of deep depravity and sin but he found he could never outdistance God.

> I fled Him down the nights and down the days;
> I fled Him down the arches of the years;
> I fled Him down the labyrinthine ways
> Of my own mind; and in the mist of tears
> I hid from Him, and under running laughter.
> Up vistaed hopes I sped;
> And shot precipitated,
> Adown titanic glooms of chasmed fears,
> From those strong Feet that followed, followed after.
> But with unhurrying chase
> And unperturbed pace,
> Deliberate speed, majestic instancy,
> They beat—and a Voice beat
> More instant than the Feet—
> "All things betray thee, who betrayest Me." [2]

This happens in personal affairs. The ancient psalmist knew that God calls us to reckoning from which we cannot escape.

> When I declared not my sin, my body wasted away
> through my groaning all day long.
> For day and night thy hand was heavy upon me;
> my strength was dried up as by the heat of summer.
> —Psalms 32:3–4

This was in the year 2500 B.P. (before psychotherapy) but way back in the dawn of spiritual awareness a psalmist recognized that God demands an account of sin and guilt. We are made so that we cannot shuffle God off so easily as we think. We can face God with contrite heart and accept His forgiveness. We can bury sin within ourselves and then support life by all kinds of defense mechanisms to handle our guilt (God's heavy hand). What we cannot do is run away from Judgment. It may not catch us until the Day of Judgment, but somewhere God overtakes us. And why not! We live in a moral universe. None of us is privileged.

What is true in personal affairs happens also in the betrayal of justice among men and nations. Victor Hugo reflects thus on the scene prior to Waterloo:

> Was it possible for Napoleon to win the battle? We answer in the negative. Why? On account of Wellington, on account of Blucher? No; on account of God. . . . The ill-will of events had been displayed long previously; it was time for this vast man to fall. . . . Streaming blood, overcrowded graveyards, mothers in tears are formidable pleaders. When the earth is suffering from an excessive burden, there are mysterious groans from the shadow, which the abyss hears. Napoleon had been denounced in infinitude, and his fall was decided. Waterloo is not a battle, but a transformation of the universe.

We live in a moral universe where events happen "on account of God" and from this there is no escape. "If I make my bed in Sheol," said the psalmist. Earlier translators called it "hell." Whatever the original Biblical meaning of the word, for two generations we have been watching the world make its bed in hell—and behold, God is here in terrifying judgment! We make our bed in the hell of a crushing armaments race that obliterates all the best endeavors and aspirations of human souls. We make our bed in the hell of staggering injustices to the colored races and colonial peoples of the earth and now we reap the harvest of race conflict and communism. We make our bed in the hell of trying to operate government and organize the world without reference to divine support and moral justice. But by seizing control of our own destinies, calling ourselves captains of our souls, we have not got rid of God. Not by principalities and powers can we elude the Creator and Sustainer of the world, nor by making our bed in hell and disclaiming the moral sanctions. Behold, God is here in terrible judgment.

But the opposite is also true. Just as God is ever present in judgment, He is also ever with us in support of the best that we attempt. And the number is legion of people who have been able to stand in some difficult and steep place because they trusted, and found, that God was standing with them.

2. At another fork where the ways divide we face a choice that calls to question our faith concerning the ever present love of God. What will you do in the day of adversity, when some overwhelming disaster engulfs your soul? Then it is no academic matter whether or not you have drifted beyond God's reach. A woman who lay in a hospital with a broken hip following a fall down stairs had a chance to think about her life. Her family had run through a streak of what we might call bad luck. The husband and father had recently been forced to premature retirement by an unsuspected heart condition. Five years before, the daughter had been crippled with polio. To top it all off, two days after the woman's accident the garage of their home had been destroyed by fire. Her first words to her pastor when he called were, "What did we ever do to deserve all this? Why did it happen to us?"

Two years ago I was called to a home three days before Christmas to a woman whose husband and only child, a sixteen-year-old daughter, had been struck down and killed by a drunken driver as they came home from errands of love in Christmas shopping. As I came into the room I could see written all over the face of the wife and mother the cry, "My God, my God, why hast Thou forsaken me?"

And what about the life that suffers no crushing blow but simply drags on from one day to the next with no apparent meaning, no aspiration to lift it up, no joy, no adventure. "Tomorrow and tomorrow and tomorrow, creeps on this petty pace," until the person cries in despair, "What does it all mean? Why is my life such a futility?" With all of these people we stand at the fork in the road. Then it is that we say with Robert Frost, "It makes all the difference which road they take." In such moments we turn for assurance to the passages of Scripture which speak of inescapable Presence. We can give no final or real answer to their question, "Why?" But through Christ we can give them assurance that God does not leave us to drift away into the night of doubt and sorrow or defeat. If I say surely *this* darkness shall cover me, behold even *this* night shall be light about me.

In a small town in New York State during the blackest days of World War II, when telegrams from the War Department were so frequent bearing the news, "Killed in action," or "Missing in action," the ministers made an arrangement with the Western Union company to be notified when such a notice was about to be delivered. They were not given the contents of the message but were advised that bad news was about to come to a certain home. When the news had been received a messenger of God came with the assurance of love and friendship, the word of strong faith. Usually little could be done in the immediate moment of shock, but it gave witness to the seeking love of God even in the darkest valleys of death. Even more direct, bearing witness to God's initiative and His seeking love, is the way one minister sought a friend in the valley of trouble. A man had lost a son in a tragic accident; grief had brought him near to his wit's end. He was on the verge either of suicide or ruin by alcohol, but the minister kept seeking him in the blackest hours, going to his home when some inner sense sounded the warning of great need, finding it "necessary" to go to New York at the same time the man journeyed there on business, and keeping just close enough to him so he knew he was watching him, but not invading the man's private life. The man confessed later that this minister, who represented God to him, had pulled him back from the pit. Through him he was sure of a God who goes where we go and suffers what we suffer.

No darkness is too great for Him. The greatest darkness in all the earth, the darkness of Calvary, was not too great for God. Jesus cried, too, in that darkness, "My God, my God, why!" But he trusted God beyond the darkness. Looking at Jesus and knowing that he suffered there for us, seeing in him the limitless love of God, people have lost the fear of darkness. It was for our sakes that God sent Christ into the world, and if God loved him and stayed with him through his Calvary on account of us will he not also accompany us through whatever Gethsemane and Calvary life compels us to endure? If God be for us, He will. Jesus' last words were "It is finished," and "Father, into thy hands I commend my spirit." As Elmore McKee once expressed it, "These are words of utter conviction. Holding fast to love, in spite of the misgivings of his mind, he had been holding fast to God." If there is someone listening now in gross darkness, feeling he has escaped from God's love, the word of our gospel is to you as it was to Jesus: Holding fast to love, whatever your misgivings, you are holding fast to God. At such a fork in the road to which we all come we recall the words of Whittier:

I know not where His islands lift
Their fronded palms in air;
I only know I cannot drift
Beyond His love and care.

3. But what about the last fork in the road from which we do not return? Faith indeed measures the difference here. But if God be with us through all the other divides in the road, if He stays with us in every darkness of soul along the way to the very end, don't you think He goes with us even beyond the end? The psalmist thought so. In a groping way, long before the Hebrews had grown to any articulated faith in eternal life, he believed, "When I awake, I am still with thee." Paul was sure of it: "I am persuaded that not even death shall separate us from the love of God." And Jesus comes to us to tell us that God loves us not for a lifetime but for eternity. "He that believeth in me shall never die." And this faith can be the redemption of life from fear and despair. Believing that the last turning of the road leads not to endless oblivion but to greater life can change every aspect of life here and now, endowing our years with greater dimensions, new meaning, and holy purpose. These can encompass, surround, and sustain every circumstance into which we fall.

John Short of Toronto tells this story which in one unforgettable picture sums up the central truth of the inescapable presence.[8] A young man was observed to enter a Roman Catholic church at lunch time and to kneel before the altar for a few seconds and then to depart. That went on for some time. The priest's curiosity was stirred. One day he stopped the young man and asked why he did it and why his devotions were so brief. The lad replied that he had to come during his lunch hour, and that he had only time for a very brief prayer before he reported back for duty. "What do you say?" asked the priest. "I say, 'Jesus, it's Jimmie,'" replied the lad. The priest was deeply moved.

Some time later that priest stood in a bedroom and, as the one who first told the story reported it, a "greater" than the priest was present. Jimmie hadn't many more days to spend in this world. The priest said he was certain as he stood there he heard a Voice saying, "Jimmie, it's Jesus."

The inescapable presence of God! When you stand at the last divide, where the ways of life part forever, if you have walked with Christ across the hills and valleys of this pilgrimage, a Voice will come from down one of the roads saying, "Come, it is I, your Lord and Saviour."

2

Because God Is Our Friend

Release from Life's Prisons

Behold a virgin shall conceive and bear a son, and his name shall be called Emmanuel (which means, God with us).—Matthew 1:23

If God is for us, who is against us?—Romans 8:31

In the Fifth Canto of Dante's *Inferno* the poet Virgil leads Dante into the second circle of Hell, where the two behold the spirits of the carnal sinners, forever driven by foul winds and furies through the black air. Two of these unfortunate souls in misery cry to Dante: "O living creature, gracious and benign, if the King of the universe were our friend we would pray Him for thy peace." It is a cry of despair that must have echoed through all the long corridors of Hell. Likewise it is a cry that has been lifted from the ends of the world across all recorded time. "If the King of the universe were our friend!" If only in this vast unfriendly creation there were some Friend or Spirit to love and sustain us.

That cry must have mingled with the other cries on the holy night in Bethlehem long ago. The Romans tried to believe that Augustus was a god and erected altars to him in the hope he would bring peace. The Jews grown bitter under tyranny longed for God to befriend them again and set them free. From deep in the subconscious minds of restless folk in Bethlehem there must have surged up the same lamentation—from the innkeeper, the tax collector, the weary peasants: *if only there were some Friend in the universe to release us from anxiety, from insecurity, from hopelessness.* The hopes and fears of all the years mingled in this cry to be heard from hell on earth: If God were our Friend!

At another Christmas more than nineteen hundred years later the cry is yet heard. A war-weary world, looking at the blackness of death, cries in agony, If God were our Friend! Lonely souls beneath life's crushing load wonder in despair, If God were our Friend! People bound by sin and links their own hearts have forged, whose hope flickers and sputters in the darkness, ask without hope, If God were our Friend? Not to the lower regions of Hell need we journey to hear this cry; we hear it at Broadway and 42nd Street, Broad and Market, Chicago's Loop, Trafalgar Square, the Champs Élysées, Church and Chapel streets. If the King of the universe were our Friend! But is He?

And then out of the blackest midnight there bursts a great light, and the music of a great choir of heavenly messengers floats o'er all the weary world, telling of good tidings of great joy. God is with us! He is for us! The King of the universe has not left us friendless in this hell. As angels bend on hovering wing hopes revive, hearts beat faster, heads lift up. No longer, *If* God were our Friend—God *is* our Friend. Joy to the world, the Lord is come. What does it mean?

1. It means first that God, the very King of the universe, is with us in darkness, in loneliness, in the prison houses of our sin. This is the meaning of Christmas, that God has entered the world to save. Emmanuel is one of the names given to Jesus; it means "God with us." For large numbers of people this has become a lost meaning of Christmas. How dramatically this was illustrated in the experience *Life* magazine had

in preparing its Christmas issue one recent December.[1] A photographer had been sent to the School of San Roco in Italy to get some pictures of the wonderful Tintoretto murals of the nativity. Arriving in Venice this photographer began his assignment. He tried to photograph these exquisite paintings in natural color. He tried with every conceivable kind of light but the colors would not come clear. Upon minute examination it was revealed that these murals of the nativity had been overlaid with four centuries of varnish, dust, and the accumulation of dirt through which the radiant beauty of the original colors could not shine. Only with polaroid light could the photographer get the paintings to come through in their authentic colors to his camera.

This is a perfect analogy to what has happened to the Christmas message itself. The real meaning of Christmas, about which the angels sang and for which the star shone, has been overlaid with centuries of sentimental varnish and commercial dust until millions see in Christmas only the sweet story of a baby in a manger for whom we are moved to pity, or the occasion for an organized, commercialized, vulgarized carnival of gaudy splendor. As one put it so sharply, inquiring about the meaning of Christmas:

> Already we are being exhorted on almost every broadcast to avail ourselves of the perfect Christmas remembrance—silk sheer nylon hose, the latest long-playing, loudest blaring jazz records, that perfect television set without which, we are warned, any child's poor life is doomed to ostracism among his playmates, the softest-tasting, the most gently inebriating scotch or bourbon. What in the world, it may be asked, has all this to do with the Advent of Christ?[2]

But if this were all, what have we on December 26? Nothing to put hope in fainting hearts. Nothing to lift the load from bending backs. But if God can shine through the accumulated varnish of Christmas to give the light of His glory in the face of Jesus Christ with the promise, "I am with you and your Friend," then hope will be ours.

In New York's Hayden Planetarium a special Christmas holiday show was enhanced by an added feature. A giant lollipop tree was projected onto the Planetarium dome, surrounded by a horizon filled with brilliantly colored toys which came to life and cavorted to the tune of "Jingle Bells." At the climax a huge figure of Santa Claus faded out in a snowstorm, and the Star of Bethlehem broke through into a sky that reproduced exactly the Palestine sky on the night of the nativity. The designer of this show may not realize that he dramatically staged the supreme Christmas message our world needs to understand: the recovery of the lost meaning of Christmas. This is not said in any criticism of Santa Claus; the effect must have delighted the hearts of all children who saw it, without doing any violence to their love of Bethlehem. But for adults it is a tragic loss to substitute "Jingle Bells" for "Hark! the Herald Angels Sing," and a lollipop tree for the manger of Bethlehem. The instinct is right to fade out these things in the light of the Christmas Star. It is about God's incarnation that the angels sang–God with us.

In *The Coming of Christ* John Masefield has given us what is probably one of the finest disclosures of Christian truth to be found in any literature. He puts the emphasis on man's *need* for Christ. The traditional nativity drama so frequently conveys little more than static stereotypes, whereas the world's awful need of Christ and God's answer to that need is the emphatic Christian gospel. In the Prologue to this festival drama Christ is represented as knowing before he came to earth what the cost would be. Yet he answers those Spirits who seek to stay his going:

> So be it, then.
> But the attempt, being worthy, should be made.
> Having beheld man's misery, sin and death,
> Not to go were treason . . .
> O brother Man, I come. . . .[3]

Moreover, the Christmas angels ought to be a vivid reminder of God's guardian angels that do not forsake us, whether at Bethlehem, or in the wilderness, or at Gethsemane. Because God is our Friend He does give us angel voices that do not fail. They were with Christ in his temptation—"Then the devil left him, and behold, angels came and ministered to him." They were with the Master in the Garden of Gethsemane—"And there appeared to him an angel from heaven, strengthening him." At the close of Maxwell Anderson's *Joan of Lorraine* Joan of Arc is condemned to die because she refuses to deny that her angel voices have really spoken to her. Just before the end, as she waits to be brought to the stake Joan exclaims: "I've heard my voices again, and I trust them. And they are good. . . . I'm glad again, and happy, even though it means I must die. There will be a little pain and then it will end. No, the pain will not be little—but it will end—and up to the end my voices will speak to me." Joan was sure that her angel voices would not forsake her at the last, and because she knew they would speak to her even to the end she did not waver at the great moment. She could face even the fire and say, "I'm happy again."[4]

The same angel voices that sustained the Maid of Orleans are with us through all the length of our days. Some person to whom I speak now faces a great hour of temptation just ahead. In every man's or woman's armor is some Achilles' heel, some vulnerable weakness which exposes him or her to frightful consequences. You know all too well what it is with you. But the Christmas gift of the gospel is this, that when in some wilderness of temptation an urge stronger than your power to resist takes you by the arm and leads you out under the fierce heat of some enticing waywardness, there comes the voice of one who loves you saying, "Fear not, my love is holding you fast." Out of your faith in God you will know in that hour that we are all bound together in one bundle of life, and there are things you will not do, and cannot do, on account of those you love. More than that, through some human angel voices you will hear a greater Voice saying, "Fear not, I am with thee." God speaks to us most of the time through the voices of those whose names we know and whose faces we love.

Another to whom these words are addressed is coming to an hour of supreme choice this year. In all the difficult circumstances of that choice your faith in God will remind you that one thing only does God ask you: to do justly, to love mercy, and to walk humbly with Him. You will know that if you do these things you can walk any road in confidence. If you do not do them no road is safe. An angel voice will speak, saying to you, "Stand upon your feet. It is for this hour that you have come here."

Surely someone close to us now is not far from the valley of the shadow of death. When someone you love goes on through that valley you need not be afraid. Your faith will see you through, a voice saying, "Let not your heart be troubled. I am the Lord of life and of death. I am with you and those you love, on this side and on the other." Because God is our Friend, these are the Christmas angels that do not "go away from us into heaven."

2. In the second place the Christmas gift of the gospel means that God has given each of us a divine identity. Parents know how children learning things by the hearing of the ear sometimes come out with amazing repetitions of what they thought they heard. One little friend, aged six, one night said a new prayer he had just learned.

> Our Father who art in New Haven,
> How do you know my name?

But the child had in truth asked doubt's most stubborn question. How *does* God know my name? With all of New Haven to look after, that question seems not entirely out of order. And how about us all, when the measure of our insignificance is not New Haven but the world? Do we not spend most of our lives inconspicuously keeping caught up to routine, nobodies so far as fame and position is concerned? A wife going about the affairs of a home into which but a handful of people come from one year's end to the next. A man working in office, shop, or laboratory, of importance only by the measure of what he produces. But if God is our Friend, He does know our names. Everybody is somebody, child of God. The humblest life takes on divine identity. God is present at the lowliest birth. God shares the loneliest life with every man who sits in darkness. Life means something when God shares it. On the birth certificate signed at Bethlehem was your name, along with that of Jesus, Son of Joseph of Nazareth.

Under the date line London, this story appeared on one of the inside pages of the *New York Times*: "A schoolboy here wrote in an essay, 'I believe so many twins are born into the world today because little children are frightened of entering the world alone.'" Give the boy credit for some deep thinking, perhaps deeper than physiology can take us. This schoolboy had it figured that a twin is God's answer to life's loneliness. He was right! In the deepest sense he was right, and his essay rated page one of every paper in the world. For one of the deepest theological meanings of Christmas is that the child Jesus is born as a twin to every child so that he will not be lonely, ever! No child ought to be lonely in our world after the birth of Bethlehem for God is "born again" in each new birth. All childhood is sanctified. This has something important to say to us about how our world treats its children. We cannot be content in a world that brutalizes its children, that condemns them to obscene homes, that starves them for lack of beauty, that victimizes them in a system that cares more for stockholders' dividends than for the bright hopes of a little child's face. If God is our Friend, then it lays upon us the divine imperative to see in every child's face the face of the Christ child, and in every human face the face of the Master. Woe to that man who by any negligence keeps a child from knowing that God is his Friend!

3. Yet once more, Christmas means that God has come into the world to bring us out of the prison houses which we make for ourselves and for each other. There must be many people who would count as the most thrilling moment of their lives the broadcast one week before Christmas in 1951 of the names of American prisoners held by the Communists in Korea. The war had been fought for a year and a half by this date, and as these names were read over the radio it was the first word that thousands of families had that their men were alive. We were later to learn that another year and a half had

to be counted before these men were actually released; some of them never lived to be exchanged. Nevertheless, even not knowing what might be the ultimate issue, it was a thrilling thing to contemplate their release from captivity. As I listened I wondered at the feelings of those who heard the names of their fathers and sons: Aaronson, Abbott, Abraham, Abrahamson, Abril, they began, and so on down through the alphabet. As the names came on my imagination took wings. It seemed to be the reading of another list of names, the names in our family, the names in our church, the names of our friends and neighbors: your name and mine on a list to be led out of the prison house. No longer the Communist prisons in Korea, but the prison house of sin and evil. The names were no longer coming from the Pentagon, but from on high. As I waited to hear my name, in one of those strange moments of revelation when truth appears sharp and clear, it suddenly broke upon me that this very thing had happened once. Long ago, on the night Christ was born, the angels sang my name, your name, the name of everyone in the world from that time forth and even forevermore.

Long before Jesus the Prophet of the Exile spoke of the Lord's Anointed in these terms: "I will give thee for a light to the Gentiles, to bring out the prisoners from the dungeon, and them that sit in darkness out of the prison house." And Jesus began his own ministry with the proclamation, "He sent me to proclaim release to the captives." This is the very heart and soul of the gospel. That thrilling revelation that came to me during the war prisoner broadcast was no hallucination of an overwrought imagination. This was the truth and the gift of the gospel. Our names were on the lips of the angels, proclaiming our release from the prison house of evil and death. For one was born in Bethlehem who could set me free, give me a new stature, a new love, a forgiveness for my sin, and a reconciliation with God. Good tidings of great joy which shall be to *all* people. That is the gift of Christmas.

The airways leading out from the Pentagon were filled with three thousand names. But the airways of Christmas are filled with the names of all the sons of men.

3

A Person-to-Person Call to God

A Way of Communication with God

> If you abide in me, and my words abide in you, ask whatever you will, and it shall be done for you.
> —John 15:7

> Tell God every detail of your needs in earnest and thankful prayer, and the peace of God . . . will keep constant guard over your hearts and minds as they rest in Christ Jesus.—Philippians 4:6–7 (J. B. Phillips, *Letters to Young Churches*)

A WELL-KNOWN business gives this assurance to patrons: "We are as close to you as your telephone." It is a good reminder; for whatever service this firm offers you have only to reach for your telephone. It is one of the ministries of the telephone that it brings so much of the world to the touch of a finger. Surely one should not accept lightly the comfort of being able in less than a minute to talk from your home to the police, the fire department, the doctor, the hospital. Is it so matter-of-fact that in the lonely hours or the great moments of life we can hear a friendly voice over the telephone and speak to an understanding heart? "We are as close to you as your telephone" is a description to conjure with. It is also a description of prayer. Through the processes of prayer God becomes no farther away than an inner telephone of mind and heart.

"Ask, and it will be given you; seek and you will find; knock, and it will be opened to you." This is Jesus' assurance in the

Sermon on the Mount. Elsewhere the Master is even more explicit. "If you abide in me, and my words abide in you, ask whatever you will, and it shall be done for you." Moreover, there is a stern logic confirming these promises of Jesus. If God be for us, as Jesus revealed in his own life, then it would be hard to believe that having put us in the world God had put Himself out of communication with us. If God is really for us, deeply and personally concerned with what happens to us, anxious to help us; if God is really the God whom we see in Jesus, whose will it is to seek and to save that which is lost, who invites men saying, "Come to me, all who labor and are heavy laden, and I will give you rest," who never leaves us but with the promise "I am with you always, to the close of the age"; if this is the God with whom we have to do, then does it seem to you that He would have left us without any means by which He could come to us, by which we could come to Him? We call it prayer, a person-to-Person call to God. This is not a general broadcast to the universe for anyone who happens to pick up the phone, or even a direct communication with a "Benevolent Purpose," or a "Principle which inheres in all things." It is personal! All the way through it is personal, a Person-to-person call from a heavenly Father at the other end of the line to you at this end. If then God is for us, giving us this priceless instrument of prayer, from it we should expect some great things to happen. What are the endowments of prayer?

1. First, and above all things, prayer brings God into the personal picture of your life. Just as a telephone call brings a familiar voice and spirit into your living room, so prayer brings God into the habitation of your heart. Even before any of the specific transactions of prayer are begun His coming casts the

whole picture into a new dimension. Christ's arrival on the scene alters the face of affairs.

Have you ever been awakened in the night by someone in your family suddenly being taken sick? Perhaps a child cries out in pain, a pain he does not understand, nor do you. And you are frightened; as the minutes go by the cold grip of terror freezes your heart. You do not know what to do, or indeed, if there is anything to do. And then a trusted doctor comes into the room, a doctor in whom you have every confidence. With no show of fear or dread he sits beside the bed and quietly takes the crisis in his hands. Somehow you are content now that he has come for you feel that he is adequate for whatever need be done. His very coming has altered the face of a dark hour in the night. So it is when the great Physician arrives on any scene of crisis.

2. Beyond any doubt and beyond any measurement Christ's arrival alters the face of sin. When prayer engages you in the act of confession to God something happens to change the face of your sin. You have to put through the call yourself, but once God has received your call of confession He takes the initiative to forgive, to cleanse, to renew your soul. No longer does your life need to remain soiled and smudged by moral failures of the past and evil dispositions of the present.

Mr. Gruffydd, the preacher in *How Green Was My Valley*, is talking to young Huw Morgan, a crippled lad confined to his bed. "Keep up your spirit, Huw, for that is the heritage of a thousand generations of the great ones of the earth. As your father cleans his lamp to have a good light, so keep clean your spirit."

"And how shall it be kept clean, Mr. Gruffydd?"

"By prayer, my son." [1]

By turning to God, asking His mercy, we have our hearts cleansed, our sin canceled. "If we confess our sins, he is faithful and just, and will forgive our sins and cleanse us." If we had no way of talking to God about our sin, no way of seeking or finding His help, the burden of evil and sin would accumulate until life itself was destroyed. Sin becomes too great a match and finally a master for a man to handle it alone. Talking to God in a contrite spirit is like making a person-to-Person call to the great Physician who can bring healing. So prayer becomes the Christian's secret weapon against the power of sin. In other sermons we shall speak more intimately about the struggle with sin; here our joy comes from knowing that through prayer we can make instant contact with One whose power is equal to the struggle and sufficient for the victory.

3. Again, Christ's arrival alters the face of affairs for others for whom we pray, about whom we talk with God. There is a moral logic here, too. Admittedly the whole matter of intercessory prayer is complex, not yielding to simple answers. Still, if God is for us, and if we are bound together in one bundle of life, then it would be hard to contemplate a system of spiritual dead ends in which our loving intercessions for others fell upon deaf ears or an unresponding heart. This does not mean that God will do what we want. It does mean that He will listen for what we need. It is the most normal thing in the world to pray for each other, beginning in the nursery with "God bless mother and daddy," and continuing to the very close of life when a man prays with all his soul for the ones he leaves behind, or at the highest summit where a person pours out his spirit for all the children of God. Difficult to explain how such prayer achieves its purpose, to be sure; yet

even harder to imagine that such prayer has no purpose and effect.

Certainly the effect of such prayer is not to inform God of something He does not already know, like the preacher in the First World War who began his invocation, "O Lord, have you seen the morning *Times*?" We may be sure that God knows all about it, understands it far better than we do, and knows what the real needs are before we put in our call. What we are doing is lifting another person up to God's care, adding our love to His love. You may say that God knows of our love already; why should we have to pray it to the other person through Him? Certainly God knows of our love, but love is a living, active thing; we do not take it for granted. A husband and wife who love each other do not presume upon that love, letting it remain unexpressed henceforth from the day of the wedding. They express it, they tell it to each other, show it to one another in a thousand ways. When we come to the wonderful fact of communion and love between two souls expressed through prayer, would you really think it would be just as real whether we prayed hard or not at all? Through prayer we are sending out all the strength of our love to the person prayed for, surrounding him with our love, and beseeching God to let the healing properties of love work within that life. It is far beyond dispute that the healing properties of love do bring recovery of body, mind, and spirit. We know not by what channels our love joins with God's love to reach the life of another. But we believe it somehow is linked with our person-to-Person relationship with God.

God makes it possible for us to help one another on the physical plane; without such helpfulness we could not survive. Why not on the spiritual plane as well? Prayer is the means of transferring that help. Let him doubt this who cares to, but experience contradicts our doubts. You know how when someone is pulling for you to do your best you find some extra measure of power you did not know you had. You know how in the dark hours of loneliness a firm hand upon your shoulder gives you the spiritual lift to get over some deep divide. You know how when once you sinned and someone forgave you it touched you with new life. Since when have we been unable to reach one another on the plane of spirit! I find it hard to believe that such communion and transfer of strength cannot happen even when all other channels are closed, even when there is no physical telephone or postage stamp to convey the message. Always there is the channel of prayer, through the ground of our unconscious mind and through the overarching sky of God's love.

Leslie Weatherhead caught hold of a central truth in these sentences:

> It is clear that in a great many matters Augustine's dictum is illustrated, "Without God, we cannot: without us, God will not." It seems that God waits for man's co-operation before certain things can be accomplished. . . . The mistake often made is that while man clearly sees that he must co-operate with God on the physical level, and thus sees the need for medicine, surgery, nursing and other means of co-operation, he does not understand that he must also co-operate on physical and spiritual levels.[2]

What do we ask of God in prayer? We say, "Father, if it be possible let this child be healed of his affliction." We say, "Lord, if it be thy will, let this man reach the goal of his striving." We say, "God, if it be her real need, answer this woman's prayer by giving some new factor." We say, "God, show us if there be any way for us to be the instruments of thy grace." And we pray these prayers with all our heart and mind and soul and strength, *and we pray them with expectation.* In every intercession is the prayer that God will surround that person or family with His love. This is the big thing: helping to pull tight the binding cords of Christian love.

Studdert-Kennedy has some wise things to say to us here:

> The first thing, by far the first, that every Christian mother should learn to pray for her son, and every Christian wife for her husband, is that by him, and through him, at whatever cost, God's will may be done. We must learn to leave the matter of life and death entirely in God's hands, and pray that in life or death our men may keep their manhood clean from every spot of cowardice or sin.
>
> Especially must we teach our children this. The first prayer I want my son to learn to say for me is not "God keep Daddy safe," but "God make Daddy brave, and if he has hard things to do make him strong to do them." . . . Daddy dead is Daddy still. But Daddy dishonoured before God is something awful, too bad for words.[3]

These were words spoken to folks in time of war. They are words for everyone no matter what the times.

4. Once more, a prayer of surrender alters the face of affairs. When in a person-to-Person call to God anyone surrenders life, puts it all in God's keeping, there is a real change. Here is the prime mechanism by which we initiate the processes leading to transformation. True, we would not seek God were He not already seeking us. In this sense God makes the first move. But on our part the first act must be that of surrender. Then God moves into the picture. In this we are following the pattern of Jesus. At the close of the temptations before Christ even began his ministry he surrendered. "You shall worship the Lord your God and Him only shall you serve," Jesus said to Satan, *and in effect to himself*. Matthew's account

reports, "Then the devil left him and angels came and ministered to him." First surrender, then the ministering grace of God. In the Garden of Gethsemane Jesus prayed, "My Father, not my will but thine be done." Immediately after this surrender Luke tells us, "There appeared to him an angel from heaven, strengthening him." Again, first surrender, then the upholding presence of God. If this is the pattern by which Jesus won his victory how much more so must it be for us. Transformation comes from surrender to One infinitely greater than we are.

Have you ever had the experience of being altogether confused, frustrated, at your wits' end, tied up in mental knots over some situation you could not unravel? You felt that if only you could call some friend and just "talk it out" it would make all the difference in the world. Or perhaps you've been bothered by some decision you had to make; you didn't know what to do, until at last you called some friend on the telephone or went to see someone face to face. Then you made the decision, a surrender of some kind, and all the face of affairs changed. Suppose you could do that with God! What a difference it would make!

You can! You can do that with God. That is what prayer is all about. Because God is for us every moment of every day He has installed a spiritual phone within our souls by which we may reach Him to surrender ourselves in every decision by which life is made. The Christian has this instrument, the unbeliever does not. In that is the largest difference between them.

Joseph Wood Krutch, writing about Eugene O'Neill's *Strange Interlude,* marks this difference as it can be seen in multitudes of people.

> *Strange Interlude* is the demitragedy of a group which neither believes in God nor wants to believe in God. In so far as the individual members believe in anything larger than themselves, that thing is the Freudian sub-conscious, some awareness of which seems to haunt them, very much as others have been vaguely haunted by an awareness of God. In so far as they "belong" to anything they belong to the "complexes" which force them into actions of which their reason would not approve.[4]

That describes a lot of people. Life becomes a dreary procession of days when we believe in and belong to nothing more than our Freudian complexes, nothing larger than ourselves. So it is a dreary affair for those who have no One greater than themselves to whom they may surrender themselves, or no means of communicating that surrender should they want to. Thanks be to God for the gift of the telephone of prayer, over which we may say: "Lord, I believe, help my unbelief. Not my will be done, but thine," and over which some sustaining word comes back from God.

An analogy to prayer suggests itself in the description of the Douglas Skynight, a new United States jet plane. This plane, says the report, "is equipped with a radar system that locks the plane onto the target in the dark." There is a million-dollar description of prayer in ten-cent, front-page words. Prayer is a spiritual radar system that locks the soul onto the target which is God, and keeps it there even in the dark. By surrendering to God and keeping that surrender in focus by prayer day after day and night after night, the heart and soul of that person can go on through the night because he is held in the grip of a love which temptation cannot divert nor tribulation destroy. Underneath the picture of this new jet plane published by one newspaper was this observation: "The Skynight has already scored several victories." So far as its spiritual counterpart is concerned I should say it had! People who had hard things to face and faced them bravely because they were not alone in the great moment. People who had bold and unpopular decisions to make and who made them without fear and no thought of favor, because they had lately been talking with One who pledged all of His upholding. What more could you ask or desire than to belong to such a company, so sure of so great victory!

4

No Fear of Tomorrow

Release from Anxiety

Therefore do not be anxious about tomorrow.
—Matthew 7:34

I am sure that . . . things to come . . . will not be able to separate us from the love of God in Christ Jesus our Lord.—Romans 8:38–39

Basil King begins his *Conquest of Fear* with this confession:

When I say that during most of my conscious life I have been a prey of fears I take it for granted that I am expressing the case of the majority of people. I cannot remember a time when a dread of one kind or another was not in the air. In childhood it was the fear of going to bed. . . . Later it was the fear of school, the first contact of the tender little soul with life's crudeness. Later still there was the experience which all of us know of waking in the morning with a feeling of dismay at what we have to do on getting up. Fear dogs one of us in one way and another in another, but everyone in some way. . . . The mother is afraid for her children. The father is afraid for his business. The clerk is afraid for his job. . . . There is not a home or an office or a factory or a school or a church in which some hang-dog apprehension is not eating at the hearts of men, women, and children who go in and out.[1]

With that analysis few of us would argue. W. H. Auden has called ours the "Age of Anxiety." Albert Camus calls this the *century of fear*. Anxiety is the most common affliction of our age. We see it on every hand—people afraid of the past, fearful of the future; people whose lives have broken down under the strain of unrelieved anxiety. Our hospitals are crowded with patients suffering from anxiety neuroses. Other millions live out their lives in the shadows of fear.

But not only do we see it in others, we know it in our own hearts. Who of us has not found himself in the clutch of gnawing apprehension and felt something of the paralysis of anxious fear? Whether our age knows more of anxiety than any other is a question we leave to inquiring minds. "Let the day's own trouble be sufficient for the day." Our concern is to know what the Christian gospel offers to the anxious soul. Jesus' words in the Sermon on the Mount remove all doubt that the Master was aware of anxiety. "Do not be anxious," or as Goodspeed translates it, "Do not worry." But to modern ears these words frequently fail to make sense. How can we help it? Real causes for worry run all the way from personal to world concerns. What about the widowed mother who sees her only son, for whom she had hoped so much, getting into bad company and going down to ruin, and all the while she seems utterly unable to restrain him? What about the young husband who finds his wife unable to adjust to married life because of a mother-fixation? Or a dependent family when the bread-winner is suddenly stricken with a fatal disease? What about the uncertainty which clouds the future of young people? What about the international situation with its economic rivalries and injustices, its ruthless wars and vaster tragedies threatening? Who can look without anxiety upon the chaos of the world?

What endowment has the gospel for us to enable a man to overcome anxiety? It is well enough to say, "Do not be anxious." But to the mother whose son is away at war, to the man who has sinned and fears discovery, to the wife whose marriage is failing, to the physically stricken father who sees his family in pathetic need—for all of these something more is needed than the admonition which they associate with lilies of the field. If God is for us what does it mean for anxiety?

1. The first endowment of Christian faith for the anxious is the discovery of what Paul called *the immeasurable greatness of God's power*. This power comes in the first instance from laying hold on God's purposes; it remains as power to walk through the seasons of anxiety. The person who has put his life in the service of values and desires that are greater than he is—that have their source in God—need have no fear of tomorrow. He has found something stronger than fear, able to subdue anxiety. Jacques Maritain has phrased it in a good way:

> Perhaps we have chosen the wrong road. Perhaps we would have done better to cling to a faith to live and die for, instead of seeking a faith to live by only. Ancient pagan wisdom knew that man's noblest, happiest, and most human aspect is appendant to what is suprahuman, *and that he can only live by what he lives for and is ready to die for,* and what is better than himself. If our humanism has failed, it is perhaps because it was centered in man alone, and was utilitarian, not heroic; because it tried to relegate death and evil to oblivion, instead of facing them and overcoming them by an ascent of the soul into eternal life; because it trusted in techniques instead of love, I mean in Gospel love.[2]

Here is the paradoxical oblique Christian strategy for release from anxiety. When deep fear lays siege to the heart the only victory is for the heart to lay siege to God's purpose. Life can take wings in the greatness of God's desires. The phrase is from Sidney Lanier:

> As the marsh-hen secretly builds on the watery sod,
> Behold I will build me a nest on the greatness of God:
> I will fly in the greatness of God as the marsh
> hen flies

In the freedom that fills all the space 'twixt
the marsh and the skies:
By so many roots as the marsh grass sends in the sod
I will heartily lay me ahold of the greatness of God.[3]

As an ancient prophet put it, "They that wait upon the Lord shall renew their strength. They shall mount up with wings as eagles." This has been the continuing experience of Christians through the ages, that when they do lay hold upon the purposes of God as disclosed in Jesus Christ they *can* mount up with wings. People have found that they could rise above anxiety when they were devoted to a Kingdom of Spirit that is greater than any little kingdoms of their own. When we make God's purpose our purpose that means the Almighty God stands behind us and within us to exceed our own strength. And our God is a great God! In His strength, in His will, we find support and power to face difficult days, to adventure into noble enterprise, to do all we can on the great day, and having done all to stand unafraid.

At the close of Alan Paton's *Cry, the Beloved Country,* on the day that Absalom Kumalo is to hang in far-off Johannesburg for the murder of Arthur Jarvis, his father Stephen meets James Jarvis, father of the murdered boy. These two men, drawn together across the racial lines of black and white by the tragedy and sin which has engulfed their sons, find reconciliation with each other in that hour of the final execution of justice. Jarvis comes to Stephen in the solitude of his vigil and tells him he will give a great share of his wealth to make green the dying valley of the Umzimkulu where the blacks live in poverty, that he will rebuild Kumalo's church, that out of terrible evil he will try to bring forth understanding and healing. Thinking of the death of the black man's son, but also of the new life in the valley, he says to Stephen: "One thing is about to be finished, but here is something that is only begun. And while I live it will continue." [4] Both James Jarvis and Stephen Kumalo laid hold on the greatness of God by entering into His purposes and discovering an immeasurable inflowing of power which redeemed the shattered remnants of their broken lives.

That is the grace of God, not only in the distant Umzimkulu, but here in New Haven, or wherever you live. On a day when you have stood amid the ruins of some disaster, sick at heart and afraid of the morrow, God can lay hold upon your life and stretch His hands over some new beginning, saying to you: "One thing is finished, but here is something new that is only begun." Anxiety swallowed up in a higher Purpose! Jesus found this way to conquer his own anxieties. "Nevertheless," he said, "I must go on my way today and tomorrow and the day following; for it cannot be that a prophet should perish away from Jerusalem." Jesus had abundant cause to be afraid—and in the simplest human terms he must have known fear for he was one of us—but fear never became anxiety because he was serving a higher purpose that consumed all anxious dread.

Ordinary common sense will recognize that one of the best antidotes for fear is activity. Get busy with something and you have less time and nervous energy to waste on anxiety. This is sage wisdom and the Christian, like anyone else, needs to apply it. But if that's all we have then we can expect the worst. If James Jarvis and Stephen Kumalo had merely come back from Johannesburg's tragedy to busy themselves with the tasks of the day they would have found neither healing nor release. It was the purpose to which they set their hearts that redeemed the anxiety of the day and the defeat of the morrow.

2. But this takes more than the power of great purpose. It

takes also the conviction of God's great faithfulness. This is the other half of our victory over anxiety, our deliverance from fear of tomorrow: because we believe that God is faithful yesterday, today, and tomorrow when it comes. Much of the anxiety of our day stems from the fact that people do not have the constant chords of God's faithfulness in the music to which their lives are set.

In that fantastic realm known as "soap opera" radio dramas depend on music to spirit listeners quickly from one scene or mood into another. John Crosby of the *New York Herald Tribune* found that the Mutual Broadcasting System has a library of ten thousand of these "bridges" running the whole gamut of emotional situations. What amazing music must have been arranged to fit these descriptive titles: *There's a Face in the Window; Quick, Follow That Car; Out of the Valley Come Slimy Crawling Things; Why Didn't You Tell Me This When We Were Back in Prairie City?* These two in particular are not hard to imagine: *Background Nostalgic—Tender Ye into Rude Awakening,* and *Light Confusion and Then Down the Stairs in a Hurry.* This bit of research suggests that all of us live our lives against the background of some kind of music, not music coming out of our radios but the music of the things we believe in, the purposes we live for, the music of our hopes, our fears, our failures, and our achievements. Is this music made up of snatches from a thousand motifs, something new to fit every oncoming episode, or are there any great recurring themes that accompany the whole of life? Even the flimsiest acquaintance with the Christian faith makes us sure of one thing: there is one mighty and sustaining theme of music that plays the background for the whole of life. One whose life is played against this music does not need to scramble around among ten thousand possibilities to find some ditty or chords that will make sense. When life is lived against the background music of God's faithfulness one does not greet each day with "light confusion and then down the stairs in a hurry." He does not inhabit an atmosphere of nostalgia, forever being broken by rude awakening. He goes on through the changes of life knowing that his life and all life belongs to God.

A man can suffer the loss of a job or the disappointment of a career and know that in the perspective of God the most important word concerning his soul has not been spoken. A person can face illness and even death in the sureness that the God who gave him life cares eternally for that life. Anne Douglas Sedgwick, the English novelist, was in her seventies when in a letter to a friend she declared: "Now, added to everything else I cannot breathe unless I am lying down. If I sit up my ribs collapse. Yet I cannot drink liquid food unless I am sitting up. Life is a queer struggle. Yet life is mine and beautiful to me. There is joy in knowing I lie in the hand of God." The joy of knowing that we lie in the hand of God dispels anxiety. We can face even the darkest and most uncertain future because we know we do not face it alone.

One of the deepest roots of anxiety in our time is the pervasive feeling of loneliness, separation from our fellows, from God, the sense of being unwanted, not needed. Auden feels it in his poem *The Age of Anxiety*,

> . . . this stupid world where
> Gadgets are gods and we go on talking
> Many about much, but remain alone,
> Alive but alone, belonging—where?—
> Unattached as tumbleweed.

> . . . The fears we know
> Are of not knowing. Will nightfall bring us
> Some awful order—Keep a hardware store
> In a small town . . . Teach science for life to
> Progressive girls? It is getting late.
> Shall we ever be asked for? Are we simply
> Not wanted at all? [5]

Not wanted at all! Life does that to human souls. It is part of the problem for which the gospel is the answer. A sense of personal significance is the gift of Christ to anyone who commits himself to him. He is a "new creature" (life becomes a new creation) who lives his life against the music of God's faithfulness.

Again, the accompaniment of God's music makes it possible for a person to be relieved of the anxiety over sin. Too often we are unaware of the spiritual infection poisoning the soul from unrepented sin. In the best of us, however, there is at least an ill-defined sense of "separation," of being "not right" with God. The only way out of this anxiety wasteland is through confession, repentance, and reconciliation. Of this we shall say more on another occasion. But if we are not sure of God to start with, we shall be forever anxious about ourselves. For this reason one of our first necessities is to keep open all the channels of communication by which God's love may overflow the innermost recesses of our souls. We can turn again to Lanier for the unforgettable picture:

> Look how the grace of the sea doth go
> About and about through the intricate channels that flow
> Here and there,
> Everywhere
> Till his waters have flooded the uttermost creeks and
> low lying lanes. [6]

God's love penetrates to the depths of life if we open every channel by which He can come in. These are the channels of prayer and constant communion. We learn to know God by living with Him, not for one anxious night but day after day. We learn to trust God by speaking to Him again and again, even when we feel that nobody is listening. We learn to feel His lifting tides around us by trying the things He has assured us will work. And always before us we have the victory of Jesus. He trusted God even through the cross. He could not see beyond Calvary but he trusted that God was there, and he threw his life upon the cross and upon God's love. He was not forsaken. If God's love was equal even to the cross, where not only Jesus' life was at stake but God's whole Kingdom, surely you can take courage for your own anxieties, even the anxiety over sin.

I devoutly wish we could close this sermon with a few neat paragraphs of simple instruction as to how to do these things easily. This sermon has led us far into a country beyond where simple homiletical maxims will suffice. In this region of life we must depend on God's grace, whose activity we do not command, but whose power we can receive. Said Rufus Jones,

> To have the whole heart and mind garrisoned with peace even in Nero's dungeon, when the imperial death sentence brings frustration to all plans and a terminus to all spiritual work, calls for some world-transcending assistance to the human spirit. Such peace is explained only when we discover that it is the "peace of God," and that it came because the soul broke through the ebbings and flowings of time and space and allied itself with the Eternal.[7]

In every anxiety while you are holding fast to love you are holding fast to God.

Could we see it best in a picture? The Golden Gate is the inlet from the Pacific Ocean to San Francisco Bay. By wind, storm, and tide this passage of water can be turned to a dangerous turbulence, churning in from the ocean. On the ebb tide, especially under a blanket of fog and darkness, small powerless boats may be carried out into trackless seas. Two decades ago engineers built a bridge across the Golden Gate. Down into solid rock beneath the bay they drove the pilings upon which the towers rose. From these towers they flung cables across the Gate, anchored in the rock on either side. From these cables they hung the bridge. For all practical purposes that bridge was built with an infinite margin of safety for stress, tension, and load. It can carry all the traffic that could be sent over it. Today people can walk unafraid across the Golden Gate through storm and darkness, because their support is anchored in the rock. Those whose lives are anchored for support in the love of God can walk without fear above the seas of anxiety across any Golden Gate to which life may lead them.

5

How Christ Intercedes for Us

Forgiveness of Our Sins

That you may know that the Son of Man has authority on earth to forgive sins.—Matthew 9:6

Is it Christ Jesus, who died, yes, who was raised from the dead, who is at the right hand of God, who indeed intercedes for us?—Romans 8:34

TOWARD the close of *Pilgrim's Progress* Christian is making his way with great difficulty upon the highway between the walls of Salvation. His enormous burden impedes his running, but over hills and valleys he struggles forward until at last he comes to a place "somewhat ascending." Upon that place stood a cross, and a little below, in the bottom a sepulcher. As Bunyan describes it:

> Just as Christian came up with the Cross his burden loosed from off his shoulders and fell from off his back and began to tumble, and so continued to do, till it came to the mouth of the sepulchre, where it fell in and I saw it no more.
>
> Then was Christian glad and lightsome, and said with a merry heart, "He hath given me rest by His sorrow and life by His death."
>
> Then he stood still awhile to look and wonder; for it was very surprising to him that the sight of the Cross should thus ease him of his burden.

Christian is not alone in this wonder. How is it, men have asked in all the ages since Calvary, that the sight of the cross should relieve us of our burdens? Truly here is one of the supreme paradoxes of the gospel: that the death of Christ on the cross, the world's darkest sin, should remain the saving secret of forgiveness. The Greeks in their wisdom called it foolishness, the Jews in their legalism stumbled at the sight of the cross. But to men who were being saved it has been the power of God to forgive sin. Still more, the clinic and the counseling room confirm the experience of Bunyan's Pilgrim. Out of his extensive experience in pastoral counseling Leslie Weatherhead of London's City Temple writes, "I have never in thirty years known a psychological treatment which, in this field of guilt, could by itself obtain freedom for the patient without recourse to all that the Christian religion offers." [1] Why? Paul gave voice to the secret when in answer to his own cry of despair—"Who shall deliver me from the body of this death?"—he prayed, "Thanks be to God who gives us the victory through our Lord Jesus Christ." *It is Christ who intercedes for us.* But why and how?

First of all we need to see that sin is a colossal defect deep within the souls of men, a situation incurable by tinkering on a patchwork basis. Among all the troubles, problems, needs that a congregation brings with them to church one above all others is ever present: the need for forgiveness. Where even two or three are gathered together, there will you find this strange need for forgiveness.

Consider this immemorial requirement as it might be found in any congregation of people. Here is a man who has become an alcoholic and through whose drinking vast shame and suffering engulfs a family. More to be helped and pitied than condemned, still this man knows that his evil has condemned the ones he loves to disgrace and impoverishment of body, mind, and soul, and in his torturing moments of sobriety he cries out for forgiveness. Again, here is a man who was entrusted with great responsibility in his job and in his community. Many people were relying on him, much was depending on him, and he let them down because of some selfish preoccupation. He sees now what a great price others must pay for his folly. He is sick at heart and wants only to be forgiven that he may make a clean start. Or, here is a man who has failed his family, deprived them of the best to which they were entitled. And so we could go on through one case after another. One glance at the situation in the waiting room where people come with this trouble should be sufficient to persuade us that here is a malady calling for extreme and profound treatment. You don't smooth away universal sin such as that, nor does one sponge it out as though he were erasing a blackboard. It lies too deep for any such superficial handling. What is more serious, none of these people can ever be whole again until forgiveness has taken place, until the burden of guilt and sin has been relieved.

Obviously they cannot forgive themselves, for while they have sinned against themselves, they have also sinned against others and it is not in their power to forgive their transgressions against their fellow men. Moreover, in the deepest sense they have sinned against God, and it is from God that ultimate forgiveness must come. Suppose some friend or member of your family whom you have wronged were to say to you, "I forgive you; now let's forget." Would that be enough? Hardly, for you would need to be sure first of all that it was real forgiveness, not just "letting you off" from your sin. Forgiveness is far more costly than that. But even where some friend has paid the full price and does forgive you, your sin still separates you from God.

I knew a man who by dishonesty in business was exposed to public scandal. He brought disgrace on his family, especially his children, who were unimaginably tortured and shamed by the immoral conduct of their father. But the family loved the man who was husband and father to them. They stuck by him through the bitter days of shame—they forgave him from the bottom of their hearts. Was this enough? Not by any reading of the affair! This man had sinned against God in violating the souls of his children, causing them to stumble and fall. Terrible damage had been done to innocent and lovely children. Only God could deal with this man's greatest sin. It was one of the Roman poet Horace's rules of dramatic art that a god must not be introduced into the action unless the plot had got into such a tangle that only a god could unravel it. Human sin is such a tangle that only God can unravel it. As the poet Horatius Bonar put it:

> Not what these hands have done
> Can save this guilty soul;
> Not what this toiling flesh has borne
> Can make my spirit whole.
>
> Thy love to me, O God,
> Not mine, O Lord, to Thee,
> Can rid me of this dark unrest,
> And set my spirit free.[2]

Only an act of God could be equal to man's immemorial need.

1. In the cross, as nowhere else, *we see first what sin has cost God.* Until we see what sin means to God we can never know the wonder of his forgiving love, because until we see that we have no way to measure God's love. If we imagine that God could easily discount our sins by simply signing an

act of amnesty it would mean that sin was not very serious, so easily to be dismissed. We know how difficult and painful it is to overcome separation between human hearts. Surely the far more frightful condition of separation from God we cannot expect to bridge in a less costly manner. That is why God could not deal with sin in any other way than to show us the cost which He Himself has suffered.

In Shaw's *St. Joan* Bishop Cauchon asks, "Must then a Christ perish in torment in every age to save those who have no imagination?" Christ has had to perish because until we *see* the cost there is no way of getting at our share of the sin. Human analogies fall far short, but again, they help us to *see* and thus *realize* the condition of forgiveness. A young man had grown careless with the hard-won support given him by his parents. They had put him through college, endowed him as liberally as they could that he might establish a home and family of his own. The gifts were wasted with prodigal disregard of their price. The man drank expensively, spent far too extravagantly, wasted his time in trivialities so that his college training amounted to little. Then his parents died; what remained of their frugal savings was his. But when his father's accounts and checkbooks were opened—records that coincided with the son's wasted years—the man *saw* the price: often a pitiful balance for his parents' necessities, hoped-for plans abandoned, savings exhausted. Life was a bleak affair for many years, redeemed only by a parents' hope in their son. And their son fouled out! Now he saw—father's and mother's love crucified by his selfishness. His life became a dedication to their hopes. They could not forgive him face to face, but through their love which lived on beyond their death reorientation set him on a new way. The parents never wanted to show their son the cost, but their love could not reach him until he saw.

Now lift the analogy to heights infinitely above the human plane (where, in this case, the father probably sinned also) and see the effect when it is God Himself in the person of Jesus Christ who takes our sin to His own heart. Take a long look at the cross. There you see the cosmic consequences of your sin, as the young man saw the human consequences of his when he looked into his father's heart. For to trace all our sins back through their tortuous intermediate stages is to come at last to Calvary where we see our sins in their true light. That is what sin does! All the sins we commit against each other reach back to the same effect: the crucifixion of Christ's love. Only as God shows us *that* can we ever be forgiven in the innermost closets of our separation from Him.

2. Again, in the cross we see not only what sin has cost God, and thus come to know how critical a need we face; we see also the *length*, the *breadth*, and the *height* and *depth* of His love. We discover at the cross a love so great that it is willing to stand and take all the shafts of evil we drive into it, and love us still. "A mighty rock within a weary land" is the way one poet phrased his faith in God. Rufus Jones has pointed out that this figure of a "mighty rock" is a poetic symbol of an actual fact well known to dwellers in desert lands. The most important single necessity that confronts people who inhabit the edges of a great desert is to keep back the drifting sand driven by pitiless winds. Sand moves like waves of the sea. Living on the edge of a desert you may awaken any morning to find that a foot of sand has buried your garden and crept to the front door sill. "The problem is to break the drift of the desert sand. A great rock or a stream of water will do it best." [3]

So does the Cross with its outpouring of God's love stand against the tide of evil in the affairs of men. It is a "drift-breaker." Tracing our sins back to their ultimate effect we do come to Calvary. But there we find Christ taking this enormous evil of the world's sin into himself and turning it to love. He absorbs the world's sin, reveals the love of God which all of our transgressions cannot weaken.

Once more, an analogy from life may light our pathway to the truth. In John Galsworthy's novel *Swan Song,* Fleur, old Soames Forsyte's daughter, in her carelessness and willfulness, causes a fire in the old family homestead. Standing beside his daughter, watching the firemen try to save some of his cherished paintings through an upstairs window, Soames suddenly sees that Fleur is directly in the path of a heavy frame about to drop. He pushes her out of the way but he himself is mortally wounded by the picture's fall. Kneeling beside her father's bed Fleur takes his hand in hers, and out of remorse and penitence over her deeds promises, "Yes, Dad, I will be good."[4] When Soames gave his life for her sinfulness, loving her at the highest cost he could possibly pay, she was redeemed and forgiven. Men have fallen on their knees in the face of a love like that and thanked God. Let's be clear about it. Neither Soames Forsyte nor the prodigal young man about whom we spoke but a moment ago *redeemed* the other person in the way Christ did. They do not substitute for God working in us. But the principle is the same. Moreover, their sacrifice would never have been made had not God first loved us through the cross.

But go from analogy to fact. What if this Father who sacrifices Himself for us is none other than God, our heavenly Father. What if He is willing to take the consequences of our willfulness and turn to us still with love! Then is the power of sin broken, for it has nowhere else to go. By His love our sin is taken away once and for all. Again, not the consequences; we have to pay for those for ours is a world of moral cause and effect. But restored in love to God, accepted as His children, the consequences become the divine discipline which we bear with glad hearts as sons of God.

For nearly two thousand years it has been the sight of the cross that has moved men to repentance, that has lifted the burdens of sin from off their shoulders. At the cross men have found "rest by his sorrow, life by his death." It was Archbishop William Temple many years ago who put it in unforgettable words: "In Christ's agony, we see what our sin costs God; and in his bearing before his enemies we see how God regards us as we inflict the blow. . . . We cannot go on wounding one who accepts our wounds like that; we are filled with fear, not the old craven fear of punishment, but the fear of wounding the tenderest of all hearts."[5] When the tenderest of all hearts stands over against the overwhelming sands of our sin and loves us still it destroys the power of sin.

3. But on the deepest level Christ intercedes for us by *bringing us back into full fellowship with our Father*. This is the critical point at which the miracle of forgiveness transpires. What troubles us most is the sense of rejection, being separated from God's love. It is a disturbing thing to see what sin costs God; still more moving to recognize His love in the Cross. But unless we are sure that we can come home again fully restored, the whole thing might be of no effect. Here is the miracle of the Prodigal Son, in the radiance of which the power of sin is canceled. When the Prodigal came home in humble penitence God threw His arms about him and brought

him into the family once more. Not in disgrace, not on probation, no longer to be punished, but loved as though no separation had ever occurred! *Acceptance* makes the difference, loosing burdens from off our backs, burdens we need carry no longer.

This great miracle of reorientation and reintegration of life Walter M. Horton once observed in what he describes as the most convincing act of forgiveness and release that ever came to his knowledge.[6] It was performed by a nurse. In one of the great hospitals they brought in from the ambulance a young woman who had been stabbed in a drunken brawl. The case being diagnosed as beyond hope the nurse was asked simply to sit with the girl until the end came. As she sat looking at the girl and thinking what a pity it was that such a face should have been marred by such hard lines the girl opened her eyes.

"I want you to tell me something and tell me straight," she said. "Do you think God cares about people like me? Do you think he could forgive anyone as bad as me?"

And the nurse says that she didn't dare to answer at first, not until she had reached out to God for help, and reached out toward the poor girl until she felt one with her. Then she said, knowing it was true: "I'm telling you straight; God cares about you and He forgives you." The girl gave a little sigh and slipped back into unconsciousness, the lines of her face changing as death approached. Something tremendous happened between God and that girl in that moment, it happened through the nurse, and, as Horton reminds us, it had something to do with what happened long ago on a certain green hill far away outside a city wall. That is to say, it was through the forgiving love of Christ that peace came to that dying girl. She was brought back into the warmth and the wonder of God's love. No other gift of the gospel ever does more than that.

In John Masefield's *The Everlasting Mercy* we have, as in few other places, the picture of a man going through this process which is at once both terrible and wonderful.[7] Saul Kane was a man utterly depraved, lecherously fastening his sins upon innocent young people and pulling them down into the pit with him. Drunken, profane, full of lust, this man was separated from God as far as the east is from the west. But one night, through the ministries of a gentle Quaker lady who confronted him in the midst of his carousing, the awful revelation of his sins was driven deep into his soul.

> "Saul Kane," she said, "when next you drink,
> Do me the gentleness to think
> That every drop of drink accursed
> Makes Christ within you die of thirst,
> That every dirty word you say
> Is one more flint upon His way,
> Another thorn about His head,
> Another mock by where He tread,
> Another nail, another cross."

In this frightful disclosure of what sin means Saul Kane's rebellion against every decent impulse was broken. He saw in the horrible light of God's judgment what he had done: children ruined, life depraved, a mother's heart broken. Oh, what a burden for one man's soul to carry.

But in the mystery of God's goodness Saul Kane did not have to carry it any longer. He felt the presence of Christ close about him!

> I knew. . . .
> That Christ was standing there with me,
> That Christ had taught me what to be,
> That I should plough, and as I ploughed
> My Saviour Christ would sing aloud,

And as I drove the clods apart
Christ would be ploughing in my heart.
Through rest harrow and bitter roots.
Through all my bad life's rotten fruits.
O Christ who holds the open gate,
O Christ who drives the furrow straight, . . .
O clover-cops half white, half red
O beauty from beyond the dead,
O blossom, key to earth and heaven,
O souls that Christ has new forgiven.

Saul Kane found that God had not forsaken him in the darkness of his sin, that he could begin again in the sonship of God's love. If there is someone to whom these words speak now who harbors in his heart the bitter roots of life's rotten fruits, you do not need to keep them any longer. Christ will plow them all under, burn them in a consuming fire, accepting you once more as his son, so that you may say with Saul Kane:

The water's going out to sea
And there's a great moon calling me;
But there's a great sun calls the moon,
And all God's bells will carol soon
For joy and glory and delight
Of someone coming home tonight.

6

When Love Has the Last Word

The Grace to Love in the Face of Sin

But if anyone strikes you on the right cheek, turn to him the other also.—Matthew 5:39

Love knows no limit to its endurance, no end to its trust, no fading of its hope: it can outlast anything. It is, in fact, the one thing that still stands when all else has fallen.—I Corinthians 13:7–8 (J. B. Phillips, *Letters to Young Churches*)

Mark Twain once wrote a story bearing the descriptive title, "The Terrible Catastrophe."[1] Before he had finished he had worked his characters into such a predicament that whatever any one of them did they would all be destroyed. Contemplating his creation at this juncture Twain concluded by writing: "I have these characters in such a fix I cannot get them out. Anyone who thinks he can is welcome to try!" That may be an unusual literary device for ending a story, but it is not an unfamiliar fix for us to find ourselves in. Again and again we discover that life seemingly has become so snarled that there is no way out. No possible word or move remains to us to unravel the knots by which life has bound us. Call it part of the price of living in a world of people that through pride of spirit, conflict of wills, and clash of ambitions our personal relations become so tangled that any move we make can only foul matters even more. If you've ever stood where harmony, mutual understanding, and respect were shattered, in a home, in a friendship, among men and women in a community, in a church, and felt tragedy and ruin all around you, you know how desperate is our need for some final word to speak that could save life.

Perhaps someone near to us now surveys his own life and sees the awful ruin of broken relationships that had been the finest achievement of his years. Someone may be crying now in bewilderment, "If God is for us, can He give us some word to speak to redeem a badly smashed communion?" He has given us such a word: *forgiveness.* Describe it as love in the face of sin. God knows we need such a resource to live without moral or spiritual defeat in a world of evil. The grace and the will to forgive at sometime in your life you'll find to be God's richest endowment, the gospel's most priceless gift.

The need and the power of forgiveness has never been spoken with greater force, except by the Master himself, than in Leo Tolstoy's familiar story "God Sees the Truth But Waits."[2] It is the story of Aksenov, who, although innocent of the murder of which he is accused, is condemned to exile for life. For twenty-six years he lived as a convict in Siberia; no word ever reached him of his wife and children.

> His hair turned white as snow, and his beard grew long, thin, and grey. All his mirth went; he stooped; he walked slowly, spoke little, and never laughed, but he often prayed.

Then one day among a band of new convicts Aksenov discovered Makar, the man who really committed the crime for which Aksenov had suffered. Makar was now exiled for some petty offense, his real murder of a quarter-century ago still undiscovered. At first Aksenov was filled with bitterness and vengeance in contemplation of his life that had been robbed from him. He tried to pray but he could get no peace. He could not go near Makar, so great was his hatred. Suddenly came his chance to strike back. Finding Makar digging an escape tunnel out of the prison he had the power to turn Makar over to certain death from the governor of the prison. Makar threatened him but Aksenov retorted:

"I have no wish to escape, and you have no need to kill me; you killed me long ago! As to telling of you—I may do so or not, as God shall direct."

When the inquiry came, however, Aksenov only answered,

"I cannot say, your honour. It is not God's will that I should tell! Do what you like with me; I am in your hands."

After this Makar came begging for forgiveness:

"Ivan," said he, "forgive me! For the love of God, forgive me! I will confess that it was I who killed the merchant, and you will be released and can go to your home."

"It is easy for you to talk," said Aksenov, "but I have suffered for you these twenty six years. Where could I go to now? My wife is dead, and my children have forgotten me. I have nowhere to go . . ."

Makar did not rise, but beat his head on the floor. "Ivan, forgive me!" he cried. "When they flogged me with the knout it was not so hard to bear as it is to see you now . . . yet you had pity on me and did not tell. For Christ's sake forgive me, wretch that I am!" And he began to sob.

When Aksenov heard him sobbing he too, began to weep.

"God will forgive you!" said he. "Maybe I am a hundred times worse than you." And at those words his heart grew light and the longing for home left him. He no longer had any desire to leave the prison, but only hoped for his last hour to come.

In spite of what Aksenov had said, Makar confessed his guilt. But when the order for his release came, Aksenov was already dead.

Between these two men love had the last word, and in its speaking the wounds of sin and evil were healed. They could not have been healed in any other way. How clearly Tolstoy has gotten hold of this fact! God does see the truth but even God must wait for the grace of forgiving love. Aksenov needed to be healed of the sins of bitterness, hatred, and vengeance, however innocent his suffering was. Makar needed to be healed of the sins of pride and cruelty. The only way that healing could come to either of these men was by forgiveness. Only a forgiving love could reach and change Makar's cruelty; his heart was unassailable except by love. And only the act of forgiving could bring peace to the one who was wronged. It doesn't make sense, does it? At least not in the terms we're accustomed to having make sense! An innocent man, twenty-six years in prison, unable to find peace until he forgave the man who shattered his home and his life. But when he did the miracle happened. Whenever the relationships between people are mangled by sin as they were here, forgiveness is the only way by which these lives may be restored to wholeness again. Here is something that must go beyond all systems of justice. Here is why the person who stubbornly insists on retributive justice never gets out of his blind alley.

What about this strange weapon in the arsenal of love by whose grace even the snarls of sin can be untied and life restored to life in the harmony of God's love?

1. The first thing we ought to avoid with scrupulous care is thinking that forgiveness makes up the damage sin has done. No one can make that up, not even God. The innocent prisoner Aksenov forgave Makar, his crucifier, and Makar at the end came and fell down pleading for mercy and forgiveness. But that did not bring back those twenty-six years of living death in a lonely exile. Nothing could do that.

During a recent Christmas season the following story appeared in a weekly magazine.[3]

Marion Davies arrived in Richmond, Virginia, with her husband Horace Brown to meet his family. One of the first points of interest was the First Precinct station, former headquarters for Brown when he pounded a beat on the Richmond force back in the early 1930's. Dressed in diamonds and new $15,000 mink coat . . . Marion went on a tour of the lockup. At the sight of some thirty small-time crooks and drunks sleeping it off, the Christmas spirit struck. Marion offered to foot the fines for all concerned and empty the jail. The magistrate explained that such wholesale amnesty was impossible.

If such amnesty is impossible in Richmond's jurisprudence it is surely impossible in God's justice. Sin has a price that no sentimentality can rebate. Recall the familiar words of George Eliot's *Adam Bede* to state the case in a sentence. Adam discovered that Hetty Sorrel had been shamed by Arthur Donnithorn. The girl's ruin can never be mended, try as Donnithorn may to set things right. He goes to Adam and begs forgiveness; Adam gives it but reminds the transgressor, "There's a sort of damage, sir, that can't be made up for." Sin and broken relationships leave a sort of damage that can't be made up for, even when all is forgiven. We ought never to misinterpret the doctrine of forgiveness to mean a simple process of canceling all consequences and setting everything to rights. The results of our sins remain with us even after we are forgiven.

2. But if love's last word in the face of sin does not cancel sin's effect it does open the way to a new creation. Because love spoke a last word through Christ in the presence of evil, God could say—even after Calvary—"The former things are passed away; Behold, I make all things new." It is in love that new creations are born. From love of men and women comes the mysterious power to create life. Out of the artist's love for the perfect ideal come the great creations of the mind

and heart, music, writing, art. Because men and women loved home and country have come the heroic acts of sacrifice that have created the conditions for better life. When men love God come the supreme moral creations of the soul. So in our own personal relations when love speaks a last word it makes possible a new creation of person-to-person friendship in the love of God. As long as we are willing to speak words of love we keep open the way for God to take the affair in His hands and redeem it. Hatred, bitterness, coldness of heart cannot create; they destroy. But where one person can face sin with love he creates new life.

Eugene O'Neill expressed this truth in his play *Days Without End*.[4] John Loving has been unfaithful to his wife Elsa, and the discovery of his infidelity has so shocked her that she lies close to death in a crisis of delirium. Seeing the effect of his sin John's cynical composure is shattered until he is distraught with remorse and shame. But he cannot forgive himself and he cannot make it right with Elsa. Finally as the crisis approaches a priest tells John to go to the church and there to pray, asking God's forgiveness. This John wants to do, but he can't; if only God would show him that His love exists, then he would believe. But the priest tells him he cannot bargain with God. Only by seeking God's grace at the foot of the Cross will he find faith and love. At last John is able to find the temper of love coming through his prayer:

> Ah! Thou hast heard me at last. Thou hast not forsaken me! Thou hast always loved me! I am forgiven! I can forgive myself—through Thee. I can believe! . . . At last I see! I have always loved. O Lord of Love, forgive Thy blind fool! . . . Thou art the Way—the Truth—the Resurrection and the Life, and he that believeth in Thy Love, his love shall never die!

Between John and Elsa only when love had the last word could there come a new creation of their love. But O'Neill sees here to a further aspect of the truth. This love must come from a source beyond ourselves. "The wages of sin is death, but the gift of God is eternal life through Jesus Christ our Lord." Elsa's forgiveness was from God; John received it through the grace of Jesus Christ.

How does it come to us? It comes to us as it came to John Loving, to Aksenov in Tolstoy's tale, as it has greeted men across the Christian ages: through the Cross. Here God Himself faced a blank wall of sin, evil, and rejection, but spoke a last word of love and opened the way for new creations. Men began finding that way immediately (two of them within the hour—the penitent thief and the Roman centurion), and it has gone on opening windows and doorways to new life ever since. Was there ever a home that was not saved because parents spoke a last word of forgiveness to children who hurt by their thoughtlessness? How many marriages can be counted as still full of joy and peace because one partner kept the initiative of love against sin's withering blight? How much of the day-by-day concourse of the world goes on in fruitful good will because again and again in the personal exchanges some-one spoke a word of love in the face of sin and kept an open door for spiritual associations to pass through? By pressing the initiative of love we keep with us God's chances to redeem and create.

3. Again, when one person speaks an ultimate word of love to another God's peace thenceforth guards his heart. Bitter-ness and love cannot dwell side by side in one heart. Love purges the soul of all evil intention and opens the gates to God's peace. So it happened with Aksenov: God's peace

flooded his soul like sunlight pouring into a musty cellar sealed for twenty-six years in darkness. He found peace when he spoke words of love. So it has happened wherever men and women have ventured the ways of forgiving spirit: they confirmed the psalmist's assurance, "Thou wilt keep him in perfect peace whose heart is stayed on thee." This does not mean that we shall always win a loving response to our love. The gift of freedom gives men the choice of rejecting love, even God's love. Nevertheless, love's last word does this much —with God's peace guarding our hearts *we* shall give no more occasion to stumble. Hearts may still ache for love which is scorned, but if through God's grace you can put yourself right with all men, then to the burdens of heartache will not be added the burden of sin. You will be right with God and with men; out of that comes peace which the world can neither give nor take away. In the face of love's final word neither principalities nor powers will be able to separate you from the love of God.

4. Finally, to forgive is to be forgiven. To speak a word of love yourself is to know for sure that God has spoken His word of love to you. Harold Bosley has called our attention to what a wise German scholar, Beyschlag, once said: "He who would belong to the Kingdom of Love as a recipient must belong to it as an agent."[5] Jesus put it even straighter than that. "For if you forgive men their trespasses, your heavenly Father will also forgive you; but if you do not forgive men their trespasses, neither will your Father forgive your trespasses." Call it a paradox if you will, but forgiveness of others seems to be the condition essential to recognizing our own need of love's last word. My experience of going through the pain of loving in the face of sin brings to my awareness what others must

suffer on account of me. This must ever remain one of God's great mysteries, but of this much we may be sure: here is God's endowment by which He fills our own hearts with compassion. When I have forgiven my brother for the terrible hurt which he introduced into the total sum, then I may know something of what God has done for me. Then will I know compassion in its fullest dimension and be an agent with God, "working together with him."

And out of it all grows the unassailable assurance that God's last word abides beyond all that ever happens to us, that we are never lost in sin and separation, that it is, in fact, "the one thing that still stands when all else has fallen." A girl went away to live in a strange city, work in a new and unfamiliar job, filled with fear and insecurity, in no small degree complicated by all manner of self-reproach. Desperate to hold on to something lest she sink, she sought out a minister to ask for help. He reminded her of a parable in the New Testament: a lost and lonely sheep on a steep mountainside. At home were ninety-nine sheep crowded in the fold, warm and secure, neither knowing nor caring for their member far beyond them. Just one missing—you'd have to look closely to even know the difference. But there was One who knew. A Shepherd was also on that mountainside, reaching for the lost sheep. He knew where it was. He loved it. As the girl was leaving the minister's study he gave her a copy of Alfred Soord's great painting "The Lost Sheep." "Keep this where you can see it every day. When you think the last word has been spoken concerning your life, lost in a strange place, spent by your own weakness, look at this picture and remember One who is speaking yet another word. He knows your name. He knows where you are. His peace is guarding your heart."

7

The Clemencies of God

Healing for Loneliness

I am not alone, for the Father is with me.
—John 16:32

I am not ashamed, for I know whom I have believed and I am sure that he is able to guard until that Day what I have entrusted to him.—II Timothy 1:12

"POINTS have we all of us within our souls where we all stand single." These words of William Wordsworth lay bare the human soul at one of the points where it is most vulnerable, most sensitive to hurt, most in need of support. Together with sorrow, suffering, and sin, the companion experience of separation puts faith to its severest test. It is when we stand single, lonely, naked, separated from each other, and sometimes seemingly from God, that our souls cry out, "If God be for us what does His gospel say to these things? Is there a gift of good news for the heart of loneliness?"

It would be a strange and empty gospel that had no word for the lonely. Indeed it would be no gospel at all, for loneliness invades the souls of even those whose faith is strongest, whose hearts are bravest. Actually ours may be an age of loneliness as other times have had differing psychological marks. A commentator writing about the contribution of Harry Stack Sullivan to the field of human understanding made this observation:

Whereas the chief problem in Freud's early decades *was* sexual repression, and the chief problem in the 1930's when Horney wrote *was* repressed hostility . . . there are many indications that we in the middle decades of the twentieth century are moving into the age of loneliness. The barometer portends that if we survive at all we are likely to live in chilly times, when it will be difficult to feel real warmth and meaning in our relations with our fellow man.[1]

In any case loneliness lies in wait among the shadows which attend so many of the soul's other encounters. The acute paroxysm of grief finally stretches out into loneliness. One of the effects of sin is to fill the heart with loneliness when the finer self within us asserts itself and overshadows all the rest. At supreme moments of decision, through all the crises and struggles of the soul from birth to death, we "all stand single," try though others may to share these moments with us. No wonder then that we search our gospel for its word to the lonely, to the spiritually naked.

One point where we all stand single is *where life finds us vainly clutching the severed cords of human love.* This is a point to which we all come soon or late. It is part of the price we pay for being bound together in one bundle of life where no life finds fulfillment save as it binds itself to other lives. But then when the bonds are broken! Supremely this comes to us in the separation of death. The poet George Santayana is writing about something to which few of us are strangers:

> With you a part of me hath passed away;
> For in the peopled forest of my mind
> A tree made leafless by the wintry wind
> Shall never don again its green array.
> Chapel and fireside, country road and bay,
> Have something of their friendliness resigned;
> Another, if I would, I could not find,

> And I am grown much older in a day . . .
> And I scarce know which part may greater be—
> What I keep of you, or you rob from me.[2]

There are mitigations to this loneliness; of them we shall have more to say, and folk have been granted the further grace to turn loneliness to love. But there is no luster in it, and sometimes the valley through which we walk lies long in the shadow.

But what is true of the final separation of earth we foretaste in many lesser separations which bring their own kind of pain. A child grows up and goes into the world to stand single from his parents. Jonathan long ago described it to David: "Thou wilt be missed for thy seat will be empty." A young maid moves out from the shelter of home to make her own way in a world indifferent, reserved, perhaps even hostile to her. She is alone and lonely, even though she be endowed with great inner resources. Or a lad goes off to join the army. You may see him one day at mail call, standing in the comradeship of men. But what is it in the look that marks so great a company of faces? They call it homesickness. We all stand single when we hold one broken end of life's golden cord.

Another point at which a lot of people stand single is *the point at which life passes them by*. Such a person is the grandmother of sixty-eight who said, "Every night I pray that the Lord will help me find something useful to do. My family is grown up and doesn't need me; I live by myself in a tiny apartment that takes no time to care for. I feel lost." We dwell in vast cities and millions of us are lonely in the midst of crowds, particularly the older people whom life passes by unknown and unwanted. Said Francis Bacon, "A crowd is not company, and faces are but a gallery of pictures, and talk is but a tinkling cymbal where there is not love." There is more loneliness today at the teeming crossroads of the world than our forefathers ever felt on the lonely frontier. Increasingly this has become a major social and psychological concern, knowing as we do that by 1960 one-third of our nation will be people over forty-five years of age, and one-tenth over sixty-five, not all of them lonely but great numbers to whom the experience of the psalmist will be altogether real:

> I look to the right and watch,
> But there is none who takes notice of me;
> No refuge remains to me,
> No man cares for me.
>
> —Psalms 142:4

We have social security and old-age assistance, but a minimum subsistence for the body is not likely to be confused with life for the soul.

But it is not altogether an affliction of age, this loneliness of being unknown, unwanted. Open your eyes the next time you are on a trip and stop to eat in some modest restaurant. See the people who come in alone, sit at a table and eat a silent meal, and then go out. Look at people in trains, busses, waiting rooms, on street corners and see how much loneliness is written in their eyes. How easy it is to get lost in a world that reckons its people in crowds. The wards of our hospitals, the waiting rooms of our clinics, and the pathetic procession of individuals who inhabit our institutions of welfare repeat the same sad tale spoken long ago by Ecclesiastes the Preacher: "Woe to him who is alone when he falls and has not another to lift him up." The loneliness of those who have fallen and have no one to pick them up is one of the most tragic by-products of a complex and diversified civilization. People get lost in the labyrinthine ways of impersonal social structures. A man who was nearing eighty developed a chronic ailment and had to spend the last year of his life in a hospital ward. All his life he had been a hired man on a farm; he had enjoyed a good life, among fine people, but he had worked hard. Now all his family were gone, no close friends were around to "lift him up" when he fell. Even the folks for whom he had worked were mostly dead or scattered abroad. Well cared for in the orderly and sanitary procedures of the hospital, this man was alone. On one of my visits, in answer to my question, he remarked, "Oh, I feel pretty good. But I'm so lonely!" A wistful expression . . . five words . . . but they bring the wonder, What does our gospel say to these things? Shall loneliness separate us from the love of God? Sometimes it does.

Then there is another point where a man "stands single," a point some men and women have shared with the apostles and prophets. Not to all men is this special form of loneliness sent but reserved for the most sensitive souls. Life keeps her cruelest crucifixions for her fairest spirits. There is a loneliness which always comes to *men and women who in the name of righteousness or peace, and for God's sake, stand against the tide of popular thinking,* who contradict the prevailing mood and temper of their times. This is what Jeremiah was talking about:

> I have become a laughing-stock all the day . . .
> For the word of the Lord has become for me a reproach and
> a derision all day long.
> Why did I come forth from the womb to see toil and sorrow,
> and spend my days in shame?

What hurts the most is not the general situation of standing on unpopular ground, but the loneliness of being rejected and scorned by those whose love and respect is the sum of life. The psalmist knew this,

> Insults have broken my heart, so that I am in despair.
> I looked for pity but there was none; and for comforters but I found none.

Jesus knew it. When he stood up to preach at Nazareth they said, "Is not this Joseph's son?" And when they heard what he had to say they were filled with wrath and drove him from their midst. Such has been the hurt of Christ's followers in all the ages, to be called unbalanced, ridiculed, laughed at. To be insulted and driven by our enemies brings suffering enough, but it is hell's own delight to have a man's own family, his closest friends, his associates whom he most needs misunderstand, misrepresent, and deliberately persecute. There is more than a suggestion in Mark's Gospel that Jesus' family never really understood what he was doing and may even have tried to "restrain" their brother. The devil has concocted a whole catalogue of ingenious ways of driving the sword through the heart, all the way from mental and emotional cruelty to innocent children, through social ostracism and "black-balling," to the pinnacle of self-chosen loneliness: "They all left him and fled . . . and there they crucified him." This is part of the loneliness of the Cross. And it is part of the promise of Christ to everyone who takes up a cross to follow him. Despite what ill-informed opinion would sometimes have us think, God's promises are not good news of sweetness and light for the comfortable and the pitiable and the weak. They are promises of loneliness and rejection. The loneliest souls of earth are the strong, the very courageous, the unflinching ones who dare to stand with the prophets and Jesus. They are the ones who want some report about what to say to loneliness and rejection. It is to these people that Jesus spoke in the summit of the Beatitudes, "Blessed are those who are persecuted for righteousness' sake, for theirs is the kingdom of heaven."

At one more place we all stand single: *the place where we seem to stand naked against a hostile universe. Man Stands Alone* is the title of a book by Julian Huxley. At the heart of this philosophy is the belief that man is a curious, incongruous by-product in a universe utterly indifferent to his plight or even to his presence—a tale that is told, full of sound and fury but signifying nothing in the universal scheme. Only in the far country of sin can people ever become more thoroughly lost than when they face the overarching sky with no faith in God above it, than when they face a silent grave with no hope for life beyond it, than when they pass through some fiery trial and feel no love within it, than when they pass through the deep waters and feel no ground beneath them. If you have ever stood in any of these places you know how single has been your standing. What shall we then say to all these things? Are there any *clemencies of God* here?

The phrase is from Amos Wilder in a poem called "Thanksgiving."

> Thanks though we be cast off, unknown, alone,
>   Thanks that we are well known,
> And though our outward man and lot decay,
>   The spirit kindles day by day;
>
> Thanks for the faith that sees beyond these snows
>   The clemencies of God, the lily and the rose,
> Beyond these graves, these ruins and this waste,
>   A garden of men, an empire undisgraced.[3]

Lovely poetry, but is it true? As true as any words can be! These lines are but another expression of the assurance that the loneliness of all who follow Christ has been, is, and will be redeemed. There are everlasting clemencies of God, as ancient as the ways of God with men, as timeless as the stars in their courses.

1. One of them is the assurance that God, the good Shepherd, seeks us when we are lost. Everyone who has ever been found by the seeking Shepherd will give testimony to the saving difference between being alone in the spiritual waste places of life, with no one either knowing or caring, and being alone but sure that the great Shepherd of the sheep knows where we are and what is happening to us, and comes seeking us when we are lost. Indeed, more than knowing or caring, this Shepherd comes to us and stays with us. Most common among all the feelings which attend loneliness is the conviction that no one understands. Says the person who is lonely: no one in all the world knows how I feel. And he is right! Being human as we are, and standing single as we do, no man can ever really suffer the heartache of another. For great numbers of people life consists largely of the "pain of stifled things."[4] But the good news of God is that there is One who does understand, that these stifled beauties and longings of our hearts are not beyond the attention or the understanding of God. This knowledge will never take away all pain. It is not a pair of rose-colored glasses or a spiritual sedative that God offers us in loneliness, but a knowledge that He cares, and that knowledge holds us back from the final plunge into despair. Only by a loving heart can a man be saved when he stands alone.

This was vividly portrayed in Albert Camus' novel *The*

Plague. The plague may be thought of as the symbol of many things in the life of man. The scene of the story is a city in North Africa isolated by an outbreak of the plague. No one may enter or leave the city for a long period of time. People die by the hundreds; those who survive grow weary and sick at heart. One of the characters while looking into a shop window at Christmas thinks in despair of his wife's face. He has not seen her for so long and quite probably will not see her again. A doctor who is witness to the scene perceives the truth behind the sad picture. "He knew what the old man was thinking as his tears flowed and thought it too: that a loveless world is a dead world, and always there comes an hour when one is weary of prisons, of one's work and devotion to duty, and all one craves for is a loved face, the warmth and wonder of a loving heart."

That man, standing in loneliness, gazing into a store window, his heart reaching out for love, might be a fitting symbol of our own situation. But as the doctor perceived what we all crave—a loved face, the warmth and wonder of a loving heart—so did he also describe in memorable words God's way with us in loneliness: not to amuse and distract us with all kinds of things, but to redeem us by a loved face and the warmth and wonder of His loving heart. There is a loved face even when circumstances quarantine us from all that we love most; there is the warmth and wonder of a loving heart, even in life's coldest winter of isolation. "For it is the God who said, 'Let light shine out of darkness,' who has shone in our hearts to give the light of the knowledge of the glory of God in the face of Christ." Living in a world where evil is never conquered, where each is a prisoner to some plague, and where all stand single, only such a love exceeds the limits of man's despair. Things are of no avail; even people may not help much unless something more comes through them.

> When some beloved voice that was to you
> Both sound and sweetness, faileth suddenly,
> And silence, against which you dare not cry,
> Aches round you like a strong disease and new—
> What hope? what help? what music will undo
> That silence to your sense? Not friendship's sight,
> Not reason's subtle count; not melody
> Of viols, nor of pipes that Faunus blew;
> Not songs of poets, not of nightingales
> Whose hearts leap upward through the cypress trees
> To the clear moon; nor yet the spheric laws
> Self-chanted, nor the angels' sweet "All hails,"
> Met in the smile of God: nay, none of these.
> Speak THOU, availing Christ—and fill this pause.[6]

God has filled this pause in Christ.

2. Again, by setting before us great and holy purposes, allegiance to which fills this pause in lonely souls, God transmutes loneliness into love. The person who can realize, even when he is bereaved, while he is rejected, though he may be despised and suffer personal crucifixions which leave him standing alone, that even, and especially, here there are supreme values to be secured, ultimate causes to be supported, commanding loyalties to be served—this person will not go down in the final defeat of despair. Life still has meaning for him for God has given him something to do which is ultimately worth doing, come what may. This is no slice of the old advice, "Keep busy and you'll forget your troubles." That is poor advice to start with because keeping busy and forgetting are not what we want. Our loneliness and rejection are bound up with our finest loves and highest loyalties. These we would

never forget even if we could, no matter what pain they bring us. Not a case of distracting our attention and forgetting our pain, what is really called for here is a matter of serving some higher and nobler purpose which includes the loves for which we mourn, or the loyalties for which we suffer, or the pain which circumstances have thrust upon us.

One of the finest transmutations of loneliness into service was achieved by Oliver Wendell Holmes in the last six years of his life. On April 30, 1929, Fanny Holmes, wife of Justice Holmes of the Supreme Court, fell asleep in her room after many weeks of mounting fatigue and steady ebbing away of strength. As he left her Holmes surmised that she would never waken again. Nor did she, for death came that evening at the age of eighty-nine. Three days later she was buried in Arlington National Cemetery. Here are the words Catherine Drinker Bowen used to describe Holmes in that hour.

There was no one in the house now but the servants and John Lockwood, Holmes' secretary. In those weeks, alone with the Judge, young Lockwood saw philosophy tested in a hard hour. Often, Holmes had talked of life and death, saying gravely that life was action, the use of one's powers. And now, with half his life snatched away from him—and there was no possible doubt that this woman had been half his life—the Judge went serenely on. The routine did not break, the work was done hour by hour. It was like the routine of a soldier, inexorable, accomplished moment by moment in the face of death itself. Simply, the Judge was living out his philosophy.

A case had come up in the Court concerning freedom of speech: The United States versus Schwimmer. Holmes knew which way the majority would vote—and with every drop of his blood he disagreed. Sitting at his desk he examined the briefs and evidence. . . . Rosika Schwimmer had been denied citizenship. . . . She was a pacifist . . . fifty years old. She had testified that in case of war she would not bear arms.

Holmes pushed aside the papers, reached for his pen: "*If there is any principle of the Constitution that more imperatively calls for attachment than any other it is the principle of free thought—not free thought for those who agree with us but freedom for the thought that we hate. . . . I would suggest that the Quakers have done their share to make the country what it is. . . . I had not supposed hitherto that we had regretted our inability to expel them because they believe more than some of us do in the teachings of the Sermon on the Mount."*[7]

When the case had been handed down Holmes rode over to the cemetery as he was to do so often during the six years of life that remained to him and placed a flower on Fanny's grave. Then he stood silently. Holmes turned his hour of supreme personal denial into an hour of supreme affirmation, affirming in bold language the ideals for which he and his wife had lived. Each of us in some degree can transcend loneliness in affirmation; it may not be on the Supreme Court of the United States, but it will be before the Supreme Court of eternity, where life will be judged not by the notoriety of the work we do, but by the integrity we bring to it and the way in which we affirm those everlasting purposes of God. In the loneliness of the Upper Room Jesus affirmed, "I am not alone, for the Father is with me." God turned Jesus' loneliness into the heroic saving act of love by which all other loneliness is now redeemed.

3. Another clemency of God is closer to us than breathing, nearer than hands and feet. It is God's gift of a whole world of spirit in which to dwell, in which to find continuing satisfaction through the years, even when we stand single, stripped and naked of life's outer defenses and bulwarks. One of the tragic aspects of life beyond the ages of sixty and sixty-five is the steadily diminishing area that brings satisfaction and fulfillment to so many. This is not apparent at twenty-five, or thirty-five, or forty-five while we enjoy full health and vigor.

Life is so full of a number of things; we can keep ourselves amused, distracted, engaged, busy with things and absorbed with possessions. What if these are but for the moment? In the next moment we can move on to something new. But then comes the day of impaired health and suddenly our physical activity is restricted. Then comes the day of retirement and we find much time with little to do. Then comes the day of reduced circumstances and we can no longer pursue pleasure. It is a terrible thing to discover ourselves with meager spiritual resources. So far as life's inner cupboard is concerned, when the hunger of frustration, boredom, and loneliness sets in many people find themselves like Mother Hubbard, going there to get some bone that will bring easement. And they make there the discovery that hit the poor dog in the nursery rhyme—the cupboard is bare and they face the prospect of life's shrinking to a further futility.

Part of the loneliness and futility of advancing years comes from "finding ourselves" in terms of a great abundance of things possessed, and then discovering that we have lost life itself. We have lost our souls when we have lost, or never even found, the capacity to enjoy God, the joy of renewing our spirits in worship and prayer, the reward of doing for others without ulterior motive, the satisfaction of serving a commanding purpose that overshadows prudential considerations. The fact that great numbers of people hardly know what we're talking about here when we mention enjoying God only indicates how much we have come to think of life in terms of a sum of things, possessions, activities, amusements, pleasures, and how little we regard it as a profoundly spiritual affair in which the main business is something transacted within the soul of a man between himself and God.

Thank God for the clemency of a world of spirit which time, adverse circumstances, and loneliness do not blight, a world of spiritual reality to which we may go again and again to renew our souls. Nakedness of possessions, fearfulness of facing life in strange surroundings separated from familiar faces need never separate one from God if he has found His companionship in previous days and kept it through the years. "Thanks . . . though our outward man and lot decay, the spirit kindles day by day."

A good exercise for every younger person to undertake would be to ask himself the question: How well am I prepared for the inevitable later years of adjustment? To find the answer project your life straight on ahead twenty, or thirty, or forty years. Assume that you could set your life down on a drawing board, and then by means of ruler and compass extend it on into the future just as it is. What would it look like? What do you do in your spare time? (There used to be something known as spare time! If you had it again what would you be doing with it?) What continuing satisfactions do you find in life beyond the changing pleasures and excitements of the moment? Can you find re-creation for your spirit in music, in reading, in the arts, in the enjoyment of nature? What rewards and benefits do you draw from spiritual life, prayer, worship, communion with God? Will these things be sufficient to sustain life in older years, or in days when you must stand single?

When Abraham Lincoln said farewell to his friends in Springfield when he left for Washington he gave the whole event a reference to God: "Trusting in Him who can go with me, yet remain with you, and be everywhere for good, let us confidently hope that all will yet be well." In some unmistakable way that whole scene is tinged with loneliness. His was the loneliness of leaving old friends, of taking heavy responsibilities whose burdens few could know or share. Yet the great purposes of God to which he had related his life hovered above his loneliness, the communion of spiritual things which had steadied his life undergirded his singleness. He found consolation and strength in the presence of One who could go with him, yet remain with his friends, and in all places be a power for good. If you have learned to know this God you will have no reason to fear the dawn of any day that ever comes.

4. There is still a fourth clemency of God for the follower of Christ from whom life has robbed some dear possession and who now stands single. We have already found out that ours is a God who never leaves or loses us, that He has set great purposes before us in the doing of which He translates loss into love, and that God surrounds life with a realm of spirit that is able to sustain even life's greatest loss and most adverse denial. Now we find at the summit in Jesus Christ the promise that in and through every denial and lonely crucifixion of love there is a redeeming power at work, making for righteousness, goodness, and love in the life of the world, if we will let it work in us. Here is a conviction to which every lost and lonely soul can hold fast, come what may: a God who through denials, broken hearts, crucifixions is yet redeeming His world. Hell has no power against this because this God takes the very instruments of hell and uses them to redeem and refine and make perfect. The Jews were denied their homeland and Mount Zion itself, carried to Babylonian captivity where "by the waters of Babylon, there they sat down and wept, when they remembered Zion." Yet by these same

waters of Babylon they found God to be greater than they had ever known Him. Jesus was denied the understanding and love of his own countrymen, even his closest friends and family. "He came unto his own and his own received him not." Yet through the loneliness of Gethsemane came the God to whom Jesus was soon to say, "It is finished. Father, into thy hands I commend my spirit." Paul was denied every crowning benefit with which his life of faithfulness might have been rewarded. But from a Roman prison while he awaited a martyr's death he wrote to Timothy, "I am not ashamed, for I know whom I have believed and I am sure that he is able to guard until that Day what I have entrusted to him." Though all things were taken away, Paul trusted them all to God and this persuasion gave him spirit to go on. Even his loneliness he entrusted to God.

Something greater was in and through all of these denials. Someone redeemed them. But they had a common secret:

"If I do not set Jerusalem above my highest joy. . . !

"Not my will but thine be done. . . !

"It is no longer I who live but Christ who lives in me. . . !"

There is a power conserving, blessing, supporting the best things which God puts in your life, no matter what the world may give or take away.

But let's be honest about this business of being faithful to the bitter end while we abide all denials. It is very easy to mistake sheer stubbornness for undeviating faithfulness. It is always easy to imagine that we are in the Garden of Gethsemane when as a matter of fact we have simply wandered away in the night and have neither intelligence nor humility enough to turn around and come home. One of our favorite psychological mechanisms by which we bolster ourselves up and rationalize our failures is to convince ourselves that everyone is out of step but us. So it is easy to console ourselves in the midst of scorn by some waters of Babylon saying, "God loves me. God is in favor of my plan. Just wait till God vindicates the day, see who pays the bill." Well, as a way of exhausting our spleen and bolstering our self-respect this may be satisfactory. But those are not the primary goals to be attained, and the difficulty is that it gets in the way of learning and offends humility. Most of all it just simply may not be true. God may not approve the way you live your life at all. The frustrations and attendant loneliness may in fact be evidence of His judgment, the means by which you are called to repent and seek God in some other way. There is uncertainty and a great margin for error when we file a claim upon God. We have no claim upon God, and any claim we make puts us in error to begin with. There is a better way.

We can appeal to God's mercy, humbly asking not that He confirm our will but that His will be done in us. And having done that we can trust the God who stands within every shadow. It ceases to be a matter of being vindicated by God and becomes a matter of God's love seeing us through while we have breath in our body to serve Him. Jesus on the Cross was not thinking of how the Cross would prove him to be right and confound his oppressors. He was forgiving his tormentors and thrusting himself upon his Father's mercy. He was trusting a loving Father whose love reached him in the most lonely exile to which a man was ever condemned. And he found that the God to whom he had trusted all the rest of his life was to be trusted with life itself, and even greater than his own life, his Kingdom.

No more does the follower of Jesus Christ need to fear the

loneliness of the Cross, or the emptiness of denial, or the blank frustration of life's closed doors. There is a love beyond those things, and there is healing in the knowledge that God forever guards the things which belong unto His Kingdom, even the humble offerings which we make. "I am sure that he is able to guard what I have entrusted to him until the great Day."

8

But If We Suffer with God

Redemption of Suffering

Jesus began to show his disciples that he must go to Jerusalem and suffer many things . . . and be killed, and on the third day be raised.—Matthew 16:21

We are children of God . . . provided we suffer with Christ in order that we also may be glorified with him.—Romans 8:16–17

FROM Job to Oscar Wilde is a long stretch of time, space, and attitude. It was Job in the Old Testament who cried in the midst of adversity, "Though he slay me yet will I trust Him." Half a century ago Oscar Wilde remarked that there is enough suffering in one London lane to show that God does not love man. Between these two men lies a great gulf. The distance between them measures the magnitude of the problem which suffering presents. So great is the mystery of suffering, so variously has suffering dealt with men that it has called forth every rejoinder from the unswerving devotion of Job at one pole to embittered atheism at the other. In fact, such is the burden of the mystery we confront here that those who have been suffering's most troubled witnesses long since have learned that on these grounds only silence becomes a man. Beyond the assurance of support and friendship anything we say will be at the very least improbable, more likely impertinent, and at the worst impious.

Consider: In a book called *Karen* Marie Killilea writes one of the most soul-moving stories ever told by a mother.[1] It is the story of her daughter, for the first few months of her life seemingly like any other child. Then her parents began to notice disturbing little signs indicating that perhaps all was not well with the little girl. They took her to a doctor. When he had finished with his examination he said to the parents, who had told him they could adjust to any fact, "Your child has spastic paralysis, or more properly speaking, cerebral palsy."

"What does it mean?" Mrs. Killilea almost shouted the question.

"I was told in medical school," said the doctor, "that a cerebral palsied child would never sit up, use his hands, or walk."

What would you want to say to that mother at that moment? What would you want to say day after day as she was told by a parade of doctors that cerebral palsied children have no mentality, and then came home to look into the bright, eloquent, alert—sometimes pleading—eyes of the little girl which spoke of a sweet soul in bondage?

Consider: Not long ago a husband and father went off to work at his job in a near-by factory. During the night while he was away a fire broke out in his home. The storm windows he had recently hung all around the house provided such perfect insulation that the house soon became like an oven. What would you say to that man were you the one to go and tell him his wife and eight children had burned to death?

Or consider the anguish of the prophets in all ages, from Jeremiah weeping for Judah, "Is there no balm in Gilead? Is there no physician there? O that my head were waters, and my eyes a fountain of tears, that I might weep day and night for the slain of the daughter of my people!" to Woodrow Wilson, a man broken in health and spirit, seeing the defeat of the League of Nations, the crushing of his life hopes for America, and the forewarning of greater tragedies which he never lived to see—this has been the suffering of the great ones.

From these we could go on to a thousand and one refinements of suffering. Each one to whom these words come could write his own chapters of suffering. In the face of such vast pain, such cruel anguish it is better that we hold our peace. But we cannot in so doing put a leash on our minds, for whether we like it or not we cannot get rid of these questions. From the beginning men have wrestled, and they must wrestle, with the problem of suffering, for it challenges our faith that life is divinely ordained and it lays bare and sometimes threatens our very existence. There is a good deal that has been said, much that might be said about pain of all kinds, some of it flippant nonsense spoken by fools who barged in where even angels held their peace. On the other hand worthy things have been said that are worth our hearing, that help to cast light upon dark mystery. I direct you to others wiser than I who have written on the why of suffering, the wherefore of human and natural evil. But ere one has advanced far into this realm of pain he discovers that the question is no longer why? but how? It has ceased to be so much a matter of "Why do I suffer?" and become the issue, "How can I get through?" The need of one struggling through the valleys of suffering is not for an explanation but for a power. The man who is lost in the wastelands of sorrow and pain cries out not for reasons but for rescue.

Moreover, people in the midst of darkness are not primarily concerned, if at all, with argument and complaint. What they seek lies in another direction altogether: someone to help them out of their trouble. A man overboard in a lake half a mile from shore is not caring at the moment about why the boat overturned, or whether he should have been there at that time, under those conditions. What he wants to know is, "Can I swim to shore, and if not, is there anyone to rescue me?" Job may have started with remonstrance with God, but before long we hear him cry, "Oh that I knew where I might find him." Jesus began his prayer in the Garden, "Let this cup pass from me"; before he had drawn another breath he continued, "Not my will but thine be done." He turned to another who held the key to Gethsemane and Calvary. Paul was afflicted in every way. He tells us that three times he besought the Lord about some personal weakness that it be removed. But Paul's mind, far from being occupied with argument and complaint, turned rather to cry, "Abba, Father. Who will deliver me from this body of death?"

And so it is that we look not for arguments to satisfy the inquiring mind but for resources to sustain the fainting heart. And through a window of faith we see beyond the valley to the hills from whence cometh our help. Paul says, "Provided we suffer with Christ we may also be glorified with him." The great Danish philosopher Kierkegaard wrote a book with the amazing title *The Gospel of Suffering*. In other words, the good news of suffering—what kind of presumption is that? Suffering, good news? Is not this the dark and brooding mind of the melancholy Dane of philosophy? Suffering obviously is news of evil report, we say. Sometimes it is altogether tragic. But seen through the window of Christian faith this report of Kierkegaard begins to make sense, for if we suffer with God then suffering can be the occasion for good news.

1. First of all there is good news in the discovery that, as we suffer with God, *He suffers with us.* This is not good news just because "misery loves company"; misery does not love company that well. Most of us who have suffered the tortures of some painful affliction, whether of body, mind, or spirit, would not have wished the pain on another, nor been glad to find anyone else in the same misery. No, in God's suffering we encounter something more than misery loving company; there is real soul therapy—great spiritual healing in the companionship of a God who shares our deepest grief, our sharpest pain, our darkest despair. For one thing it assures us that in the vast scheme of life we have not been abandoned or forgotten in the dale of trouble. For another it encourages us to discover that God does not willingly afflict us or complacently stand by as a spectator. Whatever we suffer, He suffers with us. The poet Laurence Housman saw to the heart of the matter when he wrote the lines:

> While Earth wears wounds, still must Christ's
> Wounds remain,
> Whom Love made Life, and of Whom Life made Pain,
> And of Whom Pain made Death.
> No breath
> Without Him, sorrow draws; no feet
> Wax weary, and no hands hard labor bear,
> But He doth wear
> The travail and the heat:
> Also, for all things perishing, He saith,
> My grief, my pain, my death.[2]

Talk to the ones who have come up through the vale of sorrow and their word is always the same. When God spoke to them in their grief saying, *My grief*; when God stood beside them in their pain saying, *My pain*; when God stood beside them in the approach of death saying, *My death*—then were their souls lifted up above the shrouds of gloom round about. Although we may never understand *why* we suffer it removes that suffering from the realm of meaningless affliction if God bears it all with us. For God to take our suffering and make it His personal own must have some purpose. In this we are on steadier ground than the ground of mere surmise; our appeal is to the example of Jesus suffering for all the children of God. At the very least it is a comfort to know that someone, God above all others, understands. At the very highest all things become new in the assurance that come what may nothing can separate you from God's love, that His love never sees you enter any valley alone but goes there with you, that there is nothing in all creation that you and He together cannot see through in triumph. So it makes an almighty difference that God also is looking with compassion into the longing eyes of the affected child. So it makes an everlasting difference that God stands beside the open grave. Then surely there must be some meaning in our pain that is part of a larger whole which God understands.

2. Moreover, there is good news in the discovery that, suffering with God, we can make an offering of our suffering. Psychologically this is healing: not to have to stand and "take it," like a passive pincushion, receiving all the shafts of pain which life drives into us. To be sure, sooner or later everyone comes to some hour when he has no outward course but to stand and take it. But the affair of that hour need not be settled by an outward sign you can see. Inwardly if we can offer our pain and sorrow and anguish to God we have marvelously transformed suffering. No longer is it our master but our gift. The great ones of the earth who have gone before us

turning valleys of Achor into doors of hope have left this witness: The primary thing is never the physical distress, or the mental turmoil, or even the spiritual anguish, but rather the inner response which the soul makes to these outward influences. It is an affair of alchemy in the soul, what we inwardly do with suffering, that is primary.

I'm thinking of someone now who to all outward appearance is reduced to impotence, compelled to endure the successive battering of harsh circumstances. But inwardly something far different happens each day in the life of that person. He is saying to his Lord: "God, this thorn in my flesh, this dark night of my soul is the portion life has sent me. Its mystery is past finding out. I wish it might have been otherwise. Nevertheless, I offer it to you as my gift. It is of this that you must now want me to be steward. It must be through this suffering now that I will render my account of life. Let it be a means of grace, a two-way channel between us, that you need not be ashamed of me, and that in the day of adversity I may not be found wanting before you." There is the gospel of suffering!

Hear it spoken by one who won her stripes in the long struggle against pain, Anne Brontë.

> I had hoped that with the brave and strong,
> My portioned task might lie;
> To toil amid the busy throng,
> With purpose pure and high;
> But God has fixed another part,
> And he has fixed it well,
> I said so with my breaking heart,
> When first this trouble fell.
> These weary hours will not be lost,
> These days of misery,
> These nights of darkness, anguish-tossed,

Can I but turn to Thee:
With secret labor to sustain
In patience every blow
To gather fortitude from pain,
And holiness from woe.
If Thou shouldst bring me back to life,
More humble I should be
More wise, more strengthened for the strife,
More apt to lean on Thee;
Should death be standing at the gate,
Thus should I keep my vow;
But Lord, whatever be my fate,
O let me serve Thee now! [3]

Thus, suffering, whether from divine retribution for sin, or suffering from sorrow, or pain from natural cause, can be offered as a sacrifice to God as a means of serving Him. No weary hours lost if we can gather holiness from woe. It was through suffering that Christ became one with his Father's will. It was through suffering that Job, who had only heard of God, saw God. It was through suffering that Paul became more than conqueror, a fellow-heir with Jesus Christ. Suffering, you see, can become a channel and an instrument of God's love.

It did for Karen Killilea and her mother. One day Karen asked the question her mother had dreaded from the start.

"Mom Pom, why did God make me a cripple?"

"Here it is," I thought, "and I'm not ready after all." I realized how much depended on my answer.

"I think, Karen, because God loves you better than most people," I answered slowly. "He didn't pick Marie or Rory to be a C.P.; He picked you. You have suffered already and you will suffer more. Karen, whom do you think God loved more than anyone else in the world?"

She pondered, "His mother, I guess."

"You're right, darling. He loved His mother more than anyone else, and yet He allowed her to suffer more than anyone else.

Suffering, sweetheart, is a sign of God's special love. That's why you're crippled and we are not. He just loves you more, that's all." [4]

We won't quarrel with any theology there. Who would want to soil that with fingers of interpretation? That is great faith. That is the gospel of suffering.

3. Then suffering can be good news if it leads us into closer knowledge and fellowship with God. Always one of the first effects of suffering is to strip away life's outer defenses. The security we have come to feel in the things with which we have surrounded ourselves is suddenly gone. Long ago Jesus reminded us that life does not consist in the abundance of things which we possess but in the disposition of a man's soul toward God. Despite this unmistakable word it is both the sign and the sin of our age that we seek our life and our security in the amazing number of additions we seek to add to life itself. The trouble comes when suffering of either body, mind, or spirit assails our innermost persons where the vast accumulation of possessions and psychological evasions and escapes is of no avail.

This encounter with deepest reality came to a man in a war prison camp. Some officers and men were being brutally executed by a firing squad as reprisal for recent losses to the enemy. As each man dropped to the ground the prisoner behind him became the next target for death. So the company fell one by one. The man who tells the story was saved by a last-second intervention of unexpected circumstances. But in those final moments he knew the frightful trial of stark spiritual nakedness before God as his turn came closer and closer, realizing now that all the familiar attachments of life no longer mattered. The only thing that mattered now was what his soul had to do with God. On the brink of death and eternity of what matter were the vast number of things the sum of which he had called "life"? This happened to ten thousand times ten thousand men in days of war. To a far lesser extent this is what happens in all suffering and all pain. Brought suddenly face to face we perceive our true condition. Values suddenly assume their proper dimension, as though the fog in which we dwelt had in that moment lifted and the near and distant scenes taken their true size and shape. Where is the person who has not suffered some painful failure and then looking back in remorse seen the true shape of things, the things he ought to have done and did not do, the mistakes he made which he ought to have avoided? This indeed is one of the purposes that suffering may serve, that it forces us to let go of luxuries, toys, playthings, gadgets of which we have grown too fond, forcing us back upon God until we find in Him our only abiding security and stronghold.

> All which I took from thee I did but take
> Not for thy harms,
> But just that thou mightest seek it in my arms.

So speaks God in *The Hound of Heaven.*

Of course, not automatically does this follow in the train of suffering. Some people grow bitter. Others, when forced to let go of health, or success, or hearts dear to them, do not seek the covert of God's wings but escape into private worlds of the unreal. One can derive an artificial release from suffering this way—the anesthesia of alcohol, the illusion of gaiety, other deceptions by which we keep the truth of our pain even from ourselves—but in these things is no ministry to the soul. And far be it from the purposes of this sermon to imply that the gospel answer to suffering is not a deep and abiding *joy*. A soul drooping in the deep gloom of suffering is no witness to the glory of God. But suffering must first be faced in all of its reality, and its ministry received. Then, and only then, if we suffer with God we find Him as we never could find Him in the sunlight of perfect composure or placid peace. The New Testament has no truer word than that of the writer of the letter to the Hebrews, who says of Christ: "Son though he was yet learned he by all he suffered." Suffering was God's tutor, even unto Christ. So be it, even unto us—a third sacrament, if you will, an outward and visible sign of an inward and spiritual grace.

4. At the last, one thing more at least remains to be said. Suffering is good news if it leads us through pain to larger sympathies and closer bonds with fellow-children of God. Suffering, if it is self-enclosed, all dammed up within the soul, may indeed become a poison to the soul. There is no gospel in such affliction, no gospel in mere suffering for the sake of suffering. But again, with Paul, if we suffer with God then pain becomes for us what it was for Christ: a way into the heart of God's family. Through my pain I can take my stand beside pain-filled hearts in all the places of the earth. On the cross Christ endured pain, not just for himself; he suffered there *with* and *for* all men. We speak altogether too casually about "bearing our crosses." Sometimes we make it seem almost as though minor inconveniences to our comfort had become crosses. Notwithstanding, in a profound way suffering can become for us a cross if we accept it with God, and if it leads us to suffer with all men as Christ was doing on the cross.

This is what suffering led Karen Killilea's parents to do. Out of their heartache they reached out to other parents who were likewise affected (not afflicted, in their philosophy!) by cerebral palsy, and through their efforts vast strides were made in the reclamation of human life. The tragedy of divorce could lead for many to a deeper care for the sacred institution of the home, and a fonder love for children. The bereavement of a lost partner or companion spirit could lead to a more sensitive spirit to the heart of others. The sickness of moral failure could bring a readiness to forgive in the spirit of the Master. If we suffer with God it leads to the vicarious suffering with all men, and it is by such suffering human love that we apprehend more truly the miracle of divine redemption.

Rufus Jones lost a son of eleven years who was all the world to him. He wrote many years later about the experience, concluding with this luminous parable of how his own heart was opened to God's love:

> When my sorrow was at its most acute I was walking along a great city highway, when suddenly I saw a little child come out of a great gate, which swung to and fastened behind her. She wanted to go to her home behind the gate, but it would not open. She pounded in vain with her little fist. She rattled the gate. Then she wailed as though her heart would break. The cry brought the mother. She caught the child in her arms and kissed away the tears. "Didn't you know I would come? It is all right now." All of a sudden I saw with my spirit that there was love behind my shut gate.[5]

If you suffer with God you will find love behind your shut gate, a love that can lead you through the gate to be at home with all the children of God.

9

Love Stands Also at the Heart of Death

Eternal Life

So you have sorrow now, but I will see you again and your hearts will rejoice, and no one will take your joy from you.—John 16:22

I am sure that neither death, nor life . . . will be able to separate us from the love of God in Christ Jesus our Lord.—Romans 8:38–39

Death is swallowed up in victory.
—I Corinthians 15:54

JUST as the present sermon stands at the heart of this book, so does the gift of the gospel here encountered stand at the heart of life, namely, that God's love stands also at the heart of death. David MacLennan calls our attention to a bit of poetry that lights up the ground on which we walk now.[1] One morning as Robert Browning sat at his desk, his wife softly stepped behind him and slipped a manuscript in his jacket pocket. "Please read this, and if you don't like it, tear it up." Elizabeth Barrett Browning fled upstairs while her husband read what a critic describes as "the noblest sequence ever written by a woman to a man of her choice." Hidden in the sonnets she gave him that morning are the famous lines:

> The face of all the world is changed, I think,
> Since first I heard the footsteps of thy soul

Move still, Oh, still beside me, as they stole
Betwixt me and the dreadful outer brink
Of obvious death, where I, who thought to sink
Was caught up into love, and taught the whole
Of life in a new rhythm.

That poetry can be lifted up to heights surmounting even the human love of Elizabeth for Robert Browning, and be read as a description of the difference it makes to believe that "Death is swallowed up in the victory of God's love." When love stands at the heart of death it changes the face of life, and the face of death.

1. When we know that love stands at the heart of death—as we know it in the assurance that God is for us—*it changes the face of life*. It changes the face of life's insecurities; it changes the face of life's incompleteness. Life seems insecure to most of us, and to many in the world it is savagely insecure. Having so little confidence in the safety of our souls we try to lay hold upon as many of the securities of the world as we can. The attachments of money, position, pride, recognition, and all the rest—in these do we seek the source of our consolation and insurance. They offer a deceptive protection for a while, but they are not the final harbor and in the end we have to let them all go.

Here is one of the most lovely and tender poems of our language, Coventry Patmore's "The Toys." It speaks to us of our condition.

My little Son, who looked from thoughtful eyes
And moved and spoke in a quiet grown-up wise,
Having my law the seventh time disobeyed,
I struck him, and dismissed
With harsh words, and unkissed,
—His mother, who was patient, being dead.
Then, fearing lest his grief should hinder sleep,

I visited his bed,
But found him slumbering deep,
With darkened eyelids, and their lashes yet
From his late sobbing wet.
And I, with moan,
Kissing away his tears, left others of my own;
For, on a table drawn beside his head,
He had put, within his reach,
A box of counters and a red veined stone,
A piece of glass abraded by the beach
And six or seven shells,
A bottle with blue bells,
And two French copper coins, ranged there with careful art,
To comfort his sad heart.[2]

Like the brokenhearted child, falling into sleep without the surrounding love of father, you and I gather around us these many tokens of a foolish security—tender and pitiful for a child, pathetic and tragic for us. But then Christ moves between us and the dreadful outer brink of a loveless sleep with the promise that we shall never go to sleep unloved, that we shall never die unloved. In consequence of that faith we need no longer the security of things, the attachments upon which we had childishly depended. Because we believe that death has been swallowed up in the victory of God's love, a new and final security is placed around all the edges of life. The face of life is changed when we believe there is a love that goes with us all the way to the end, and stands beyond to wait our coming. Life is delivered from its bondage to the perishables of time, for our security is untouched by time. No longer do we need to keep within our reach a box of counters, a red veined stone, two French copper coins. But as a happy child surrounded by love and security lets go his toys and the attachments of his waking hours in the faith that love guards his sleep, so may we let go of fear and anxiety. "Be of good cheer, I have overcome these things. . . . Perfect love casts out fear. . . . Death is swallowed up in victory."

Patmore's poem also speaks volumes to us of the tragedy which attends our neglect of children, that they should ever fail to feel the supporting love of God beneath them. The communication of this faith is to the subconscious mind, but it is a gift which spells the difference between fear and love over all the distance to the end. When a child lies down to sleep his faith is unknown to him, but somehow within he knows that his sleep is guarded by your love. So this life I am now living is a kind of sleep. I know that it is guarded by my Father's love, that I cannot slumber beyond His love. Death is not a sleep but a waking, and in the waking I know my Father's love will be there. This above all things I want my children to know, and if I leave them little else, possessing this faith they will be rich beyond measure. See how the face of life is changed when we are sure of God's love in the morning.

Also when death is swallowed up in victory it completes life's incompleteness. Life as we know it seems incomplete. But the gift of our faith is the persuasion that God does not leave life uncompleted. In John Masefield's *Widow in the Bye Street* the mother who has seen tragedy, evil, and sin ruin her life and the lives of those she loves most speaks of a love beyond this life, "a rest for broken things too broke to mend."

> And God who gave his mercies takes his mercies,
> And God who gives beginning gives the end.
> I dread my death; but 'tis the end of curses,
> A rest for broken things too broke to mend.[3]

With love standing at the heart of death we do not lose heart or faith; if God be for us His love will complete what the world cannot mend. The world is too full of "broken things too broke to mend" to believe in a loving God who will not or cannot heal: broken bodies, broken hearts; shattered loves and blighted hopes. Jesus knew it well when he declared, "So you have sorrow now." But he knew something more than this. "I will see you again and your hearts will rejoice." He is saying, My love waits beyond and within this sorrow; in such love there is joy that none can take away.

> All mankinde is of one Author [wrote John Donne] and is of one volume; when one Man dies, one Chapter is not torne out of the booke, but translated into a better language; and every Chapter must be so translated; God emploies several translators; some peeces are translated by age, some by sicknesse, some by warre, some by justice; but God's hand is in every translation; and his hand shall binde up all our scattered leaves againe, for the Librarie where every booke shall lie open to one another.

Surprisingly one finds also this striking paradox: Life will always be incomplete until we die many deaths. We all know the sense in which Shakespeare meant the words in *Julius Caesar,*

> Cowards die many times before their deaths,
> The valiant never taste of death but once.

It is a fair description of cowardly irresolution. It happens likewise to be a false description of a valiant life. Actually the valiant die many times before their eyelids close in the last sleep of physical death. There is no other way to live the Christian life than to die again and again. "I have been crucified with Christ. It is no longer I who live but Christ who lives in me." That was Paul's way of describing his first death. Here are some other anonymous "obituaries." I died to my own desires, in order that another person might be blessed with happiness. I died to my own pride, and forgave one who had done wrong to me, in order that our lives might be reconciled. I died to my own popularity, and spoke an unpopular opinion, in order that justice might not be smothered by silence. I died to my own will, in order that God's will might be done through me. May God have mercy on the person who cannot read these things in the summing up of his life. May He through Christ give you grace to die, to yourself, now, that you may live in Him. For be assured, my friend, that God's love stands also at the heart of these deaths. You have aught to fear. This death will be part of God's way to complete your incompleteness.

2. *This faith changes also the face of death.*

> The face of *death* itself is changed, I think
> Since first I heard the footsteps of *Christ's* soul
> Move still, Oh, still beside me as they stole
> Betwixt me and the dreadful outer brink
> Of obvious death.

The face of every death that men have ever died has been changed since Christ came between us and the outer brink. But how? Here is a mother whose son is killed in the war, a ten-year-old boy whose father dies of cancer, a woman whose husband is murdered. What about these things? What does our faith have to say to them? How does Christ come between them and the outer brink of death? When the sweetest and best we have in all the world goes down into darkness, what then? If the gospel has no gift for us here, then it is no gospel for this kind of world.

But it does have a word. We remember as Dana Burnet once put it: "God too had a Son, and sent Him into the world to contend against evil. And His enemies took Him, and hung

Him on a cross of wood, and killed Him. And His name was Jesus, who is called the Christ. . . . And the bond between God and us is the love of a Father for his children; and this love between man and God shall not pass away but shall endure forever." [4] This is what our faith is saying: When the forces of evil and sin have done their worst to the best that we know, the love of God stands beyond their power to claim. Death has no dominion over the love of God.

> War knows no power. Safe shall be my going,
> Secretly armed against all death's endeavor;
> Safe though all safety's lost; safe where men fall;
> And if these poor limbs die, safest of all.[5]

The face of death was changed for Rupert Brooke. Death is swallowed up in victory.

It is the victory of Christ that we trust here. We trust him for this final victory because he has been trustworthy all the rest of the way. It is like following a guide up the steep ascent of an Alpine summit. We trust him in many situations; we discover him equal to every emergency that meets us as we climb higher and higher. Never does he take a false step, never is he wrong in the way he guides us across ravines, over promontories, up slippery heights. He knows the mountain and he knows how to reach the summit. But then we come at last to the final ascent, where the path takes us to cloud-swept heights we cannot see. Do you now doubt the promises of the guide? Do you begin to think him untrustworthy, and assume that you know more than he? Do you, having seen him ascend every slope until now, begin to ignore his warnings, as though you were greater champion of the upper heights than he? Not if you're a real climber you don't. On the contrary, having come so far in such safe hands, you go on to the end, confident of every promise and direction which the guide speaks.

So with Jesus. He leads us unfalteringly through decisions, through crises, through higher and higher stages of life. And always proving himself the Master. Then we come to the last summit—death itself. He is equal even to that! We come here to the place where the ways divide, where we can go on not by sight but by faith. Then it is that we trust the deep invincible surmise of the soul—that a great love which stood at the parting of all other ways awaits us at the last. And if perchance we meet someone at that parting who wonders how we can go on so full of conviction, we are eager to say that because our Father met our Elder Brother at this same parting, and his death was for us, does not God still linger on the farther shore?

The face of death is changed in this conviction. Thomas Wolfe put it in beautiful words: "Something has spoken to me in the night and told me I shall die, I know not where, Saying: 'To lose the earth you know for greater knowing; to lose the life you have for greater life; to leave the friends you love for greater loving; to find a land more kind than home, more large than earth.' "[6] There is death transformed by the Resurrection footsteps o'ertaking us at the brink!

Our daughter Susan at the age of four had a favorite expression that evokes still the wonder of her childhood. Every night when I left her before she went to sleep these would be her words: "I'm going to wake up in the morning." It was a kind of orientation away from the closing day to the day which was to dawn, on which we often looked forward to some exciting adventure or family occasion for fun. In her childlike wisdom she perceived a truth: beyond the shadows of this day was a sleep, but beyond the sleep was a new morning to which she would wake. No one knows just how a child conceives time, but here was a perception that summed up both time and eternity. "And a little child shall lead them." So a little child led her father to a yet greater truth. Beyond the closing chapter of this life lies a sleep. But beyond the sleep there is a waking in a glad new morning with God. As Susan lay down to sleep in the comfort of knowing she would sleep guarded by our love and wake in the morning, so you and I can lie down to sleep at the last and, loving God and being guarded by His love, wake to Him in the morning.

10

False Gods and the Devil to Pay

The Discipline to Worship One God

> You shall love the Lord your God with all your heart, and with all your soul, and with all your mind.
>
> —Matthew 22:37

> Although there may be so-called gods in heaven or on earth—as indeed there are many "gods" and many "lords"—yet for us there is one God, the Father, from whom are all things and for whom we exist.
>
> —I Corinthians 8:6

"WHICH of the Ten Commandments would you say had the least relevance to our own present situation?" Elton Trueblood asks the question; most people would probably answer, The first two. Not because they are unimportant but because they speak to a problem that no longer concerns us. We are not polytheists, we do not worship idols. We may be lax in our devotion to the one God; we may be charged with frequent moral lapses to which the last six Commandments are directed. But we do not make graven images. So runs the popular thought on the Commandments.

There is just one trouble with that reasoning, as Trueblood has observed. It isn't true! Of all the Commandments none need to be better understood than the first two. The sad fact is that millions of people in our world are polytheists. So far as our actual working basis is concerned we do make graven images before which we bow down to serve. Jesus recognized which of the Commandments was primary. "You shall love the Lord your God with all your heart, and with all your soul, and with all your mind. *This is the great and first commandment.*" Paul was aware of man's spiritual disposition and the peril in which he stood: "There may be so-called gods . . . indeed there are many 'gods' . . . yet for us there is one God." And in our own time modern man needs to learn nothing so much as the truth that the worship of false gods leads to disaster. Many of the gifts of the gospel of which these sermons speak we receive as inner reinforcements, divine consolations, a spiritual grace that redeems life from destruction. Here is one endowment which is primarily discipline rather than dispensation. If God is for us, if He really cares about what happens to us, we may be sure that the first thing He asks of us is the spiritual discipline to worship one God.

The heading for a *New York Times* review by Chad Walsh of Aldous Huxley's novel *The Devils of Loudun* was this: "False Gods and the Devil to Pay."[1] It states the case for this sermon in seven words. We live in the kind of universe where a man's moral and spiritual orientation brings its own reward and exacts its own price. There is the devil to pay when we no longer worship the one God who is above all and in all, and begin to render homage and devotion to lesser gods, creatures of our own heads, hands, and hearts. What are the false gods, the golden calves which we worship at the foot of Sinai?

1. The first false god which commands the worship of modern man is a secular order of life, a culture whose ideals and institutions put God politely to one side. This secular culture no longer sees as its first duty the exaltation and service of God; by implication it makes itself god. The creations of our culture are the gods we serve, along with the spiritual goals required to defend these creations, rather than letting God

establish and ordain the values which our culture ought to conserve. To put it another way: Although outwardly we may keep the religious trappings of life, and even indulge in a good measure of personal piety, our actual working loyalties are to economic structures, social ambitions, political parties.

Sometimes the gods of secularism take the form of material possessions. "Get all you can. Life consists of the abundance of things we possess." Heaven knows—and so does hell—the world is heavily populated with this kind of thing. This false god has the devil to pay for sure. The price is high, so high that in the piling up of possessions we lose our soul. But this is secularism in its simplest form. Only the most stupid of fools goes for this appeal (there being a great population of fools in the world). I do not like to appear to speak with too much authority about the devil but I imagine that even he ceases to be much carried away with this temptation. He has a far more lucrative game to play where the stakes are higher. Secularism, life with God left out, can be much more subtle than mere slavery to possessions, and therefore much more dangerous. Here is where the devil gets in his real licks and pulls up the net with his greatest catch.

Our gravest peril is in making religion a thing to be put off in one compartment of life—something in which to engage apart from the rest of life, as though by a process of fission we had shattered life into a great number of compartments and then put religion into one of them. Some time ago the heading for one of the *New York Times* editorials read, "Time Off for Religion." It referred to a Supreme Court decision on released time for religious instruction in the public schools of New York. Entirely apart from the content of the editorial, in four words that heading defines the central issue of our times: what will happen to a nation and to a culture when religion becomes a sideline for which we take time off from the supposedly more important affairs of life?

Our peril lies in this: Not only have we put religion off into a compartment and thus ceased to make the worship and service of God the primary obligation for the whole of life, but in its place we have substituted the worship of half-gods. We glorify ideals and institutions which are basically good but which when separated from all religious reference and Christian sanction end in futility and corruption. These half-gods are actually more dangerous than the threat of a ruthless tyranny such as communism in the same way that the accommodation of the religion of Israel to the gods of Canaanites was more serious than the threat of Babylonian captivity. Religion always emerges sure and strong from times of crisis and challenge. The worship of half-gods is subtle; most of the time we do not realize what we are doing. Our worship is of things superficially resembling Christianity, or of things which have attached themselves to Christianity in such a way that we no longer clearly distinguish between them. When these half-gods are separated from their religious roots they are as dangerous to our life as a pagan invasion.

Here is the heart of the problem. In politics and government, in business and social life, in education, in our moral life, commendable as our conduct may often be, we are not motivated primarily by religious impulses. That is to say, *we do not seek first the Kingdom of God*. The directives of the Christian gospel are not the primary sanctions which the average American obeys. We may attend church in greater numbers now than ever before in our history, and we may pay lip service to the Christian faith. But our primary commanding allegiance is to other things. We believe in democracy in government; we believe in free initiative in business; we believe in freedom from restraint and dogma in education; we believe in freedom from authoritarian control in the social organization of life. These are the primary loyalties and ideals which we serve—the half-gods of American religion. For the most part they are good. Unfortunately many of us do not know what the score is on these things, nor do we realize that they are down for the count of ten unless something sharp and radical is done. Trueblood has accurately diagnosed our difficulty: "We are trying to maintain the dignity of the individual apart from the deep faith that every man is made in God's image and is therefore precious in God's eyes. . . . We are trying to keep the notion of freedom while we give up the basic convictions on which freedom depends."

For example, democracy would be impossible apart from the Christian faith in the worth of every person because he is a child of God. The Christian gospel produced and nourished democracy, even though we admit that democracy is not perfect and ought never to be made equal to the Kingdom of God for it is possible to have a Christian society under other forms of government. But let democracy become a god—an end in itself—and it soon falls captive to other ends. That is precisely the deep trouble that we see now in every capital of government. Our government and our democracy were established by men of profound religious faith. The very language of the Declaration of Independence and the Constitution of the United States claims a higher sanction for what they established than the mere creation of a political state. "To establish justice, insure domestic tranquility, promote the general welfare"—these purposes speak from the Preamble of the Constitution. The Declaration of Independence is founded upon the faith that all men are endowed *by their Creator* with certain inalienable rights. Our whole democratic system roots in an estimate of man as of intrinsic worth because he is a creature of God, and our government was established to be an agency that would make possible the realization of that worth. *In other words, there is a religious reason for democracy.* Our trouble today is that we no longer think of democracy as being religious, having lost its religious purpose. Unconsciously too many of us think of government as an institution to serve some other purpose than the general religious welfare of men—and I use the word *religious* here to mean men's economic, political, social, and moral welfare as children of God. Corruption in government comes from this betrayal, the corruption of men who give and accept bribes and milk the public treasury, and the corruption of the deep religious purposes of government by all men and groups who look upon the government as an agency to be used to secure some private gain or selfish advantage. The powerful labor unions seeking to manipulate government often in an irresponsible way to secure partisan advantage; the National Association of Manufacturers and the United States Chamber of Commerce, under the cloak of "free enterprise" which they make into the great American religion, seeking to secure partisan advantage from the government; the American Legion, the farm bloc, sectional lobbies and so on up and down the land until democracy has become a struggle between parties and pressure groups for vainglory and advantage. This is the real corruption in government—the corruption of the religious spirit of democracy.

What has been said of our democracy could be said with equal truth of our business and professional worlds, and of our social patterns, which dominate the lives of so many, even as the Hebrews were enamored of Aaron's golden calf. No matter what we say with our lips our behavior makes it clear that our religious allegiance is to false gods—and there is the devil to pay for this allegiance. One thinks of it as a crazy "house of mirrors" so frequently found as an attraction at amusement parks. The victim finds himself caught in an intersecting maze of passageways paneled with mirrors. Every avenue of escape leads only to a bump on the head and the reflection of ourselves in another mirror where we thought was a door. The difference between that and our secularism is that *no way* leads out of the maze in which we are caught. No door leads to freedom. The only way out is through a power that can break down the walls and lead us across the barriers. In society, in democracy, in our material achievements, in every order of secular life we shall see only the reflection of ourselves. It is when such a power as we find in Christ takes hold of us and lifts us up that we shall be delivered. When a great loyalty to God puts all other loyalties in its own service, then have we freed ourselves from false gods. It is then on a religious basis that our problem must be met, turning from a half-god to the God who is the Father of our Lord Jesus Christ, receiving from Him the discipline and the reward of worship.

2. St. Paul said there were many gods. He was not mistaken about either his own world or ours. The sacred cow of our secular culture has delivered herself of a great family of golden calves. One of the most golden is the hope of salvation by science. The past twenty-five years have done a pretty good job of pulling the rug out from under the extravagant hopes we once had in the power of scientific achievement to save us. Led by the scientists themselves, thoughtful people have come

to recognize that far from being an escalator leading to a roof-garden paradise science can be an elevator plunging us to the depths of hell. Men have lost faith in the power of science to bring them or their world either peace or security. In fact the marvelous capacity of science has brought us all to the edge of deep anxiety. But like the fable of the Sorcerer's Apprentice we have let loose such forces of destruction that we cannot now speak the word to control them.

Nevertheless, despite our rational and perceptive misgivings as to what scientific genius can and will do to the world, the temple of the golden calf of science is thronged with worshipers. Although anxiety grows unabated by science or gadgets and real deliverance remains afar off, men seek their *practical salvation* in everything from supersonic speed to automatic dishwashers. The real tragedy cast by these things is not in the greed or the perilous power which they represent but in the paganism which they call forth, substituting the gods which our heads and hands have brought forth for the God who is the Creator of all things. We would not admit to this pagan worship but pathetically our lives give unmistakable devotion to mechanical inventions, automatic contraptions, and a way of life that cannot function without them. One of the gifts of the gospel gives us to see here, as elsewhere, that only on a religious basis–making all things subject to our worship of one God–can the problem be met.

3. Side by side with this golden calf of scientific salvation is the idol of education. It casts us beneath the same peril. When we begin to worship the false god of mere education without reference to the profound convictions of our Christian faith, which motivated the movement for public education and which give point to education, we wade into the quicksands of

paganism. "Now hold on a minute," says someone; "let's be intelligent and not get hysterical over this." All right. But, my friend, if you think it is way out of bounds to call the worship of education pagan, stop for a minute and take a good look. A professor of philosophy at one of our great universities, speaking at a recent Conference on Higher Education, voiced the thought of many when he asserted that spiritual values are of no concern and should be no objective of education. "We must leave them in the magnificent isolation and solitude," he declared. And so what happens? Religion is made a thing to be encountered on the side, if at all. Meanwhile the main stream of learning and experience for millions of our youth goes on as though religion and spiritual values had nothing to say in all the areas of life that shape our destiny. If that doesn't accurately describe paganism then language has lost its meaning!

Earlier decisions of the Supreme Court held that the first amendment of the Constitution meant that religion could not in any way be an affair of public education. How far we have come from the spirit of our fathers! Subsequently Justice Douglas wrote an opinion concerning New York schools which brought encouragement to many. He upheld the right of students to study religion in released time when he said: "We are a religious people . . . and when the state encourages religious instruction . . . it follows the best of our traditions. . . . We find no constitutional requirement which makes it necessary for government to be hostile to religion or to throw its weight against efforts to widen the effective scope of religious influence." Great words are those from the Supreme Court, words turning us away from paganism toward education of our children.

But that is only part of the problem, and a small part. Released time is a good thing; religious courses in the curriculum are all to the good, the more the better. *But religion must be all through education.* Education must serve a religious purpose—*not sectarian, or dogmatic! but religious*—in the recognition that spiritual values are real, that they do have something to say to every area of life, and that our lives do have a cosmic significance. Education which deliberately side-steps this responsibility, pretending that it is a subject on which to remain neutral, is pagan education. Aaron's golden calf in all its shining glory!

Again, only as religious motives direct our efforts will we find our way out of this wilderness. George Buttrick brought the most striking statement of the matter to our attention in words from the National Council of Independent Schools:

> The disestablishment of churches in the United States was not intended to interfere with the faith of the people of the United States in a Supreme Being. When the country was founded it was written into law and established in custom, that while there was to be separation between the powers of the state and those of the churches, and while each American was to be protected from compulsory worship with any sect or creed, and while the right of any man to dissent according to his own conscience was guaranteed, the reliance on God and trust in Him were to be recognized and perpetuated. *Thus the source of our ultimate security and unity is an understanding of man's position in relation to eternal reality and participation in the resources of faith. This is the spiritual heritage to which our children are entitled.* [Italics mine.] [2]

4. Another golden calf in the herd of false gods is the idol of power and security. We are on a frightening merry-go-round. The more power we have the greater our anxiety, but the more anxious we grow the more desperately do we clutch for more power and security. The crisis comes when we reach

the point where our primary need is for internal direction and moral control rather than accumulation of more power. Sir Arnold Toynbee has discovered this pattern in his *Study of History*. He suggests that every civilization reaches the point where the challenge shifts from the external to the internal sphere. The transition from a physical challenge to a moral challenge has been the occasion for many downfalls. Speaking of one of the rulers of ancient Egypt Toynbee writes:

> Would he play the generous part of Prometheus in Aeschylus's drama or the tyrannous part of Zeus? We know the answer. He built the Pyramids; and the Pyramids have immortalized those autocrats, not as ever-living gods but as grinders of the faces of the poor. . . . As a nemesis for their misguided choice death laid his icy hand on the life of this growing civilization at the moment when the challenge which was the stimulus of its growth was transferred from the external to the internal field. In the somewhat similar situation of our own world today, when the challenge of Industrialism is being transferred from the sphere of technique to the sphere of morals, the outcome is still unknown, since our reaction to the new situation is still undecided.[3]

We are at that point now: whether we can recognize and accept the moral challenge implicit in our physical power. As the poet Lilith Lorraine put it:

> When planes outsoar the spirits, flying blind,
> When ships outsail the dreams that gave them birth,
> When towers dwarf the upward reaching mind,
> When wealth is mightier than simple worth—
>
> We almost hear the turning of a page,
> We almost know what every seraph knows,
> That somewhere on a universal stage
> A tiresome play is drawing to its close.[4]

good

To continually resist the lure of the false god of power we need a religious mastery of the moral directions of that power, which mastery can come from nothing save the worship of God Almighty.

What then must we do? We must repent of the way in which we have yielded to the worship of half-gods and false gods, and in that repentance get our house back on its religious foundations where we seek first the Kingdom of God, which ordains all other loyalties with their true value. Consider this striking description of where the trouble lies that must be healed. V. A. Demant, Canon of Christ Church, Oxford, sums it up:

> The human situation at every point is the result of an intersection of two forces, man's link with the place of his origin and the place of his fulfillment which Christians call God, *and* his alienation from it. The alienation is not due to his being an earthly, finite, limited and historical creature, for he is these things by creation; it is due to the propensity in him to give some aspect of his relative and limited existence an absolute and infinite value. It may be his mind or his spirit, then he follows the sin of Lucifer; it may be his possessions, or vital urges, then he seeks to relapse into the stream of Nature. . . . Or it may be one valid part of his communal life—like his race, or state, or class or economic devices—that is assumed to be that which gives significance to all the rest.[5]

But these partial aspects of our lives will remain out of control until we get things right in the up-and-down dimension of life in which men are related to God. The Christian task is not primarily to extend the horizontal dimensions of wealth, property, security, or social welfare, education or knowledge, or to "pour moral oil on the world's creaking machinery," or to think that if the machinery is redesigned all will be well. Our task is that of investing our loyalties with their true value and their proper perspective. To do this we must go beyond repentance, deepening our own worship and commitment. Deeply in our own personal lives we must reach out to touch the eternal power of God, in prayer, in worship, in a loving community of people.

Sometimes to do this will mean to renounce many of our holdings in the kingdoms of this world. Sometimes to do this will bring us face to face with God "on the steps of night." Gregory found this in Robert Raynolds' novel of the fall of Rome, *The Sinner of Saint Ambrose.*[6] In the tragic fate of his daughter, murdered in the death throes of Rome, in the intensity of his wife's sufferings and the failure of his own life "was the piercing presence of God on the steps of night."

> Our whole age [concluded Gregory], our whole Roman world, had gone dead in its heart because it feared tragedy, took flight from suffering, and abhorred failure. In fear of tragedy we worshipped power. In fear of suffering we worshipped security. In fear of failure we worshipped success. Yea, in fear of the intensity of life that is in tragedy we worshipped the coldness of death that is in power. In dread of the fertile growth that there is in suffering we worshipped the sterile obediences of security. In terror of the healing love that there is in failure we worshipped the corrupt denial of one another that there is in success. During the rising splendor of our thousand prosperous years we had grown cruel, practical and sterile. We did win the whole world. We did lose our own souls.

Gregory came face to face with God on the steps of night, not the false gods to which he had been enthralled, but the one God who heals by suffering love, the God who is able to transform tragedy and to make us victors even while civilization crumbles. Gregory found there, as we pray we may find on the steps of this night, that, fearful as it is to fall into the hands of the living God, God's perfect love casts out fear.

May He have mercy on us all!

11

Good News for a Beat Generation

An Authority We Can Trust

Follow me. . . . Whoever loses his life for my sake will find it.—Matthew 4:19; 16:25

We are to grow up in every way into him who is the head, into Christ . . . to mature manhood, to the measure of the stature of the fullness of Christ.
—Ephesians 4:15, 13

If God is for us does He have any word of good news for this beat generation? The word *beat* is not a printer's mistake. The two words *beaten* and *beat* do not mean the same thing. Speaking of the present World War II-postwar-Korean War generation one writer defines *beat* this way:

It means being undramatically pushed up against the wall of oneself. A man is beat whenever he goes for broke and wagers the sum of his resources on a single number; and the young generation has done that continually from early youth. . . . Brought up during the collective bad circumstances of a dreary depression, weaned during the collective uprooting of a global war . . . their adolescence was spent in a topsy-turvy world of war bonds, swing shifts and troop movements. They grew to independent mind on beachheads, in gin mills and U.S.O.'s, in past-midnight arrivals and pre-dawn departures. Their brothers, husbands, fathers or boy friends turned up dead one day at the other end of a telegram. At the four trembling corners of the world, or in the home town invaded by factories and lonely service men, they had intimate experience with the nadir and zenith of human conduct and little time for much that came between. The peace they inherited was only as secure as the next headline. It was a cold peace. Their own lust for freedom, and their ability to live at a pace that kills, to which war had adjusted them, led to black markets, bebop, narcotics, sexual promiscuity, hucksterism and Jean-Paul Sartre. The beatness set in later.[1]

Another word has been used to describe the generation: silent. They don't "issue manifestoes, make speeches, carry posters" or organize crusades. Youth is supposed to be confident, sure of itself, knowing most of the answers, ready to pioneer into the wild blue yonder of any frontier. This youth has little to say, is not sure even what questions to ask, and emphatically wants to keep out of the wild blue yonder.

Time magazine has indicted the generation for its "cautious desire to be well fixed." In a study of two thousand young people eighteen to twenty-nine years of age conducted by the Y.M.C.A. it was found that 76 per cent of those who discussed future aspirations were seeking primarily respectability and security: security in terms of material goods, security in terms of one's own little family circle, security in terms of acceptance and respect in one's own circle of acquaintances. One answer, possibly typical of the average, came from a young man: "The most important thing in life is to be successful, perhaps as a painter. I'd like to be happy and have plenty of money. I'd like to be married and have a nice home, kids and a good reputation in the community. I wouldn't like to be involved in politics."

Some have called this a generation without fixtures or foundations. In the study on the Younger Generation recently made by the editors of *Time* appeared this comment on the younger writers of this generation: "Most of these writers suffer from what has become their occupational disease: belief that disappointment is life's only certainty." [2] It is a generation without any great sustaining hopes. Other generations have been supported by a confident world view, by a philosophy and

theology of progress. But in the lifetime of this ge
such synthetic optimism has been caught off secon
generation has been forced into a corner, the rug
beneath its feet; it has no fixtures to stand on. *Dis*
threatening would be two accurate words to describe the world view of these people. They counter it with a great amount of calm insecurity. They've never known any other world. Threatened by the H-bomb, catalogued for military service, with no future guaranteed, inevitably life has come to seem tragically ambiguous, without purpose or pattern.

> We are the hollow men
> We are the stuffed men
> Leaning together
> Headpiece filled with straw, Alas!
> Our dried voices, when
> We whisper together
> Are quiet and meaningless
> As wind in dry grass.[3]

This generation understands what that means. An earlier generation self-consciously featured itself as "lost." This generation does not feature itself as anything. It searches rather than preaches, watches and listens rather than parades, anxious for some security to give foundation, some hope to cancel uncertainty, some faith to provide meaning. What shall we say to these things? If God be for us, does He have any gift to give here?

First of all, let us be clear about a few preliminaries. Maybe some younger people have not recognized themselves among the people we've been talking about. Perhaps your own young friends do not seem to be beat this way. These have been but generalizations about a generation. To scatter a few words about, *beat, silent, conservative,* does not encompass a whole generation. No such breezy analysis can ever take the measure of an age of youth. There is never any average individual and I suspect that there would be as many variations to the pattern as there are members in the generation. Thank God we still come as individuals, one by one, no two alike, each with his own word to speak.

Nor has this been an indictment! No one is to blame, nor are these expressed as value judgments, at this point. This is no case for praise or blame; rather have we tried to get a picture of life as it has seemed to a generation now entering adulthood. Mostly it is a picture in the generation's own words. I know that the gospel has good news for them in return!

1. The first good news is a word of assurance: The Christian gospel does have something to say to you of a beat generation. It is relevant because it offers you the only kind of security that can stand up in this world of insecurity, anxiety, uncertainty. By your own admission you are a generation looking for security, some solid basis that will give your life meaning and support. (Maybe your father and grandfather looked for the same thing, only calling it by another name.) You have found the familiar securities and supports of a former day no longer workable. The kind of faith on which your father and his contemporaries often stood for support seems altogether barren and irrelevant for the world you live in. Theirs was a faith that life was moving upward and onward; faith that if we could simply readjust the institutions of society we would be on the threshold of the Kingdom; faith that if we got rid of Hitler, Stalin, got a United Nations, evolved it into a world government, all would be well; faith that if we modified the social, economic, and political patterns

of our American Way, brought them "into harmony" with the Kingdom of God, then we could go forth to establish the new world. That reads like a burlesque today; it is just as hollow as it sounds! But we actually believed those things not many years ago. Your world has laid bare the illusions of that kind of faith. Such illusions had gotten a long way from the Biblical faith.

But if these securities have let you down where can you stand? Well, you in this beat generation ought to be able to grasp the true Biblical faith a good deal better than many companies who have marched on ahead of you. The savage illumination of atomic explosions, the shock waves of political revolutions, the turbulence of economic breakdowns have brought the world to the neighborhood of disaster and revealed for all time the hopelessness of looking for salvation in material achievement and trust in human goodness or wisdom. On the other hand these same repercussions have disposed us to look for salvation where Jesus and the prophets looked for it—*in God*! Their faith never promised them a Kingdom in terms of material abundance or social panaceas. Their Kingdom was a Kingdom of righteousness, and it came not with swords' loud clashing, or the enactments of Congress or Parliament, but by love, the suffering love of Hosea, of Jeremiah, of Christ. It was and is a Kingdom whose jurisdiction is a man's own heart. It was and is a Kingdom of relationships between a man and God, a Kingdom of communion between a man and his brothers. And this Kingdom is not at the mercy of the rise and fall of the secular kingdoms of this world, for it is not just another secular kingdom. It is a Kingdom in which you may stand firm no matter what happens to the kingdoms of this world. It is a Kingdom that guarantees you nothing, except an exile, a sword, and a cross, the very things which your world is now holding out to millions of men and women: exile from the realms of hope, a sword through their hearts, and a cross at the end of life, the crucifixion of love, honor, and peace by hate, perfidy, and violence. But you see, it is precisely because this Kingdom of the prophets and of Christ takes account of these things that it has something to say to you. It says it in terms of the supremely amazing paradox of the gospel: a crown with the cross, a crown of peace that passes all understanding, and a redemptive power that is able to overcome the evil of the world, because it is willing to love instead of hate, knowing that hate cannot destroy love. This saving power does not promise to save your skin. It does not promise you a cabinet post in the heavenly administration. There is no guarantee that you will come out top dog somewhere this side of heaven. It isn't the promise of security for the American Way of life, or any other way of life, except the way of those whose lives are anchored in God.

Strangely enough, being promised none of these things that we want so desperately, when your life is anchored in this Kingdom you will have found the one thing to which you will gladly give yourself to the limit—as one writer put it, for which you will gladly "walk on knives." As you do you will push forward to open new frontiers for the Kingdom in the life of men. Into some of these provinces the world will move, and live and be a happier place. Over others the power of evil will rise up to conquer, but in all of them you will find yourself on solid ground that cannot be shaken. God's love was not shaken by a Roman cross; rather did the cross shake the Empire. God's Kingdom is not shaken by the hammer and sickle, or the materialism that crusades under any other flag; rather do they stand under divine judgment. Add to this the assurance that your own life has an eternal dimension in that Kingdom and you have a winning word to answer your deepest prayer.

You are right when you say that life is an ambiguous affair. It doesn't fall into any neat patterns. Virtue is not always rewarded before the bar of history (at least not in virtue's lifetime!). You are right also to be acutely aware of life's tragic sense. But the moral heroes of the Bible and the men of great spiritual stature understood these things a long time ago. It is just that some of us have forgotten them. In ancient Israel, in first-century Rome men and women faced an ambiguous and threatening and tragic world like yours. There was no security there, even in grabbing "the big chance." There is no "big chance" for you now and most of you know it. That is why you grope toward some deeper security. Is this part of the reason for the resurgence of religion on many college campuses?

This deeper security you seek is in the faith of the prophets and of Jesus, an inner security that knows no fear, no anxiety because it trusts the sustaining love of God and knows that His love in a man's soul is unassailable. See how you as a beat generation forced into a corner may come out with a firmer hold on real security than did your predecessors who roamed the highways of the world in false freedom. Here is a way of life that cannot be shaken, that does encompass the darkest passages of time.

2. But if the first good news is a word of assurance, the second is a word of challenge. This security which faith bequeaths is only a ground on which to move. Out of this security you need to find the call for moral adventure. The security of faith, if it becomes no more than an inner sanctuary to

which the soul escapes from life's ambiguities and contingencies, turns out to be a sterile security. Perhaps it is a sign of greater maturity that you do not make so many speeches, issue manifestoes, lead crusades for this, that, or the other. You may not be caught off first base as often as the youth of other days. But remember, it is quite as easy to swerve off the right-hand side of the road as it is the left. It may be that this beat or silent generation has come to a greater religious awareness, driven to seek its support in the strength of an inheritance that does not fade away. But if you will examine the Biblical faith again you will see that it has two sides. It is the second side to which you are now challenged—to find a moral commitment to match your religious awareness. The only way to get out of the corner into which you have been driven is to fight your way out, and your only weapon is a firm sense of moral obligation.

The one thing you cannot say about this generation is that it is afraid of a fight. This generation is not afraid of anything. The moral futility on all sides comes not from fear, rather from the loss of a sense of moral purpose. What is there to fight for? To what are we obligated that will not let us down? At this point we would do well to hear the testimony of men who have gone on ahead, remembering that the world has not changed a great deal since their day. Oliver Wendell Holmes had this to say about life's purpose:

> Through our great good fortune in our youth our hearts were touched with fire. It was given to us to learn at the outset that life is a profound and passionate thing. While we are permitted to scorn nothing but indifference, and do not pretend to undervalue the worldly rewards of ambition, we have seen with our own eyes, beyond and above the gold fields, the snowy heights of honour, and it is for us to report to those who come after us.[4]

Life is a profound and passionate thing, as men and women whose lives have been a moral adventure have found out. There are snowy heights of honor. People have felt committed to climb toward them. Why? Because they are there! as Mallory was once reported to have given as his reason for climbing Mount Everest. Again and again has that answer come concerning other high Himalayas in the life of the race.

"Why are you committed to this job?" . . . "Because it is honorable."

"Why will you not do this thing which others ask?" . . . "Because no decent man would do it."

"Why do you fight so persistently for this ideal?" . . . "Because it is right."

This is the kind of moral commitment to which you come when you discover that life is a profound and passionate thing. It is also the way by which you make that discovery!

When William James came to the end of his long career as a teacher at Harvard he spoke these sentences as a valedictory:

> These then are my last words to you: Be not afraid of life. Believe that life is worth living and your belief will help create the fact. The "scientific" proof that you are right may not be clear before the day of judgment is reached. But the faithful fighters of this hour, or the beings that then and there will represent them, may turn to the faint-hearted who decline to go on, with words like those which Henry IV greeted tardy Crillon after a great battle had been gained: "Hang yourself, brave Crillon! We fought at Arques, and you were not there."

Those are rough words. Either you fight, or you hang yourself. One or the other, with nothing in between. But hasn't the time come for that kind of talk? Great battles are being fought for the world's destiny. Where will you be? Either you believe in a moral order whose sanctions apply to all men, everywhere, and at all times, or you believe in a despotic, autocratic order of life whose morals are made by the men in power. There is no halfway house between these two. Either you believe in the everlasting dignity of the human personality because it belongs to God, or you believe that human life is a cheap commodity to be traded for other currencies. There is no stopover on the way from one of these to the other. It is for these things that the great ones have fought. And only this kind of all-out commitment, laying life right on the line, has a ghost of a chance to fight it out with other fanatical faiths bidding for the world's loyalty.

This choice was vividly portrayed in a moving scene from Maxwell Anderson's *The Eve of St. Mark.*[5] The play concerns some men who were holding out on a small island in the Philippines in the dark days of Japanese advance during World War II. They were given the choice of staying and fighting against hopeless odds to stem the tide until they fell, or of escaping to another island and thus probably being rescued to come home. Before making the decision one of the men engages in a soliloquy with his girl back home. He imagines himself in conversation with her:

Janet:
No, you mustn't die.
What makes you speak of dying?
Quizz:
It's noon on this rock
and torrid hot, and six of us who are left
sit in the cave to vote, do we go or stay,
do we make a try for H25 and home
or man the gun while we can, fire the few shells,
sink the invasion barges, never let them in
till they've paid the last death.

Janet:
Who asks this of you?
They shouldn't ask it.
Quizz:
Nobody asks it, dear.
It's something in myself I don't understand
that seems to require it of me. It seems to be
the best of me—the same inner self that turned
to love you and love no one else, that says
give more than is asked of you. . . . But as for orders
we have none now. We're free to go back or stay
save for what's in our minds.

Later, as the six men are deciding by secret vote what they will do, one of them speaks to his fellow-soldiers saying:

Gentlemen, I find that my natural cynicism is not decreased by tropical malaria and short rations. The emotions that come boiling up out of me are not heroic . . . what difference does it make about one rock in a whole ocean, and listen fellows, we won't get another chance at the things back there we love and want to do. Who the hell picked us out to save the world anyway? And are we perfectly sure it's worth the effort? And what's the good of saving the whole world if you happen to die in the process?

But I vote to try it another day. I vote to try it another day, and probably another day after that.

There is the moral alternative, yours and mine. Every one of us is on some island of righteousness today. We can run for safety, or we can stay with it, persecuted, suffering, paying the high price of moral integrity. If you are loyal to the royal in yourself you will stay and face it. To some member of the beat generation, this day in the midst of a fight for righteousness, a fight that may cost him dearly: "Blessed are you! Blessed are you persecuted for righteousness' sake, for yours is the Kingdom of heaven." Which is to say: In losing your life in this moral adventure you shall find the only kind of life that's worth having!

3. Fine, you say, but is it true? Is God really for us? Are we not sheep to be slaughtered? Do these moral obligations to keep integrity have any real meaning?

Come now to the heart of the matter and see. The good news of assurance and the gospel of challenge are followed finally by the word of invitation. The gospel can only persuade you by inviting you to try it, to "go for broke" for Christ and see what happens. By no other way can you find out if it is true. In fact none of these things we've been talking about has any meaning at all, or any possibility, apart from a saving relationship with Christ. This is the thing that persuades. You're looking for peace, for security, for dependability. Where can you find them? How can you prove any of them so that they stand up? Not by any processes of logic. Not by any demonstrations from history. These are useful tools, surely. Anyone with a clear head will insist on using them. But they don't persuade. You'll find your peace, your security, your moral dependability only in surrender to a great love, to a holy purpose. When you've made that, with the whole world stacked against you, you can still be confident.

Paul faced your kind of world and look what was stacked against him: tribulation, distress, persecution, famine, nakedness, peril, the sword—all these arraigned against him. But in surrender to Christ he found himself more than conqueror. It is not a case of understanding all mysteries. It is a case of surrendering yourself to One whose love is greater than all mysteries. There is suggestion for the soul in the conversation of Kent with King Lear.[6] The King asks the Earl, "Who wouldst thou serve?" and Kent answers, "You."

"Dost thou know me, fellow?" asks Lear.

"No sir; but you have that in your countenance which I would fain call master."

"What's that?" queries the King.

"Authority."

That's it. There is in Christ that which we would call Master. His is an authority we are willing to trust, for which we are ready to go all out. Trusting him we find security. His authority is reason enough for moral adventure. No shaking of the foundations has altered the truth of his own words, "He that loses his life for my sake shall find it."

Through one illuminating flash does this shine clear at the close of Franz Werfel's *The Forty Days of Musa Dagh*.[7] This is the story of Christian heroism that defends something more precious than heart or home. At the end of the book Bagradian remains on the besieged land after his countrymen are evacuated. Not long after the ships sail away beyond the horizon he is shot from ambush while standing on his son's grave. In falling he clings to the wooden cross, tearing it down with him, and lies in death with his son's cross upon his heart. Is that a symbol that no life ever comes to its Christian triumph until we lie with someone's cross upon our heart? Does that mean that no church, no society, no nation can ever live in triumph until it takes upon its very heart the cross of God's whole world? Does it suggest, even more, that once for all times God took His Son's cross upon His own heart, not in dying but in living? I am altogether persuaded that it does mean these things.

The cross is God's eternal seal upon His promise that He is for us. When you take His cross upon your own heart, you'll find that He is for you, and through you, that He is for our whole world.

12

The Dimensions of God's Love

The Dimensions of Length, Breadth, Height, and Depth

I have come not to abolish the law and the prophets but to fulfill them.—Matthew 5:17

Go therefore and make disciples of all nations.
—Matthew 28:19

In me you may have peace.—John 16:33

That you being rooted and grounded in love, may have power to comprehend with all the saints what is the breadth and length and height and depth, and to know the love of Christ which surpasses knowledge, that you may be filled with all the fullness of God.
—Ephesians 3:17–19

THE visible world of space and everything in it possesses three dimensions: length, breadth, depth. The invisible world of mind and spirit knows the same three. The gift of the gospel is the will and the capacity to measure life and live it in three full dimensions. In contrast to some other world religions which seek but the dimension of height, and to the secularist, whose living never ascends from the horizontal plane, the Christian knows the abundant life when three dimensions converge in his own heart.

Hollywood's "discovery" of the third dimension, among the items of lesser importance for the year 1953, is of more than technical interest. The optics of three dimensions parallels a truth in the world of spirit. Pictures in three dimensions are pictures which create the illusion of depth, appearing as actual scenes strike the eye with the nearer objects "standing out" from the more distant background. In this they offer a striking contrast to the "flat" two-dimensional pictures. This new technique reminds many of us of older days in the parlor when the family gathered to look at the stereopticon slides, pictures which when viewed through the proper lenses assumed remarkable depth, the little images of people standing right out in the picture in lifelike perspective. (More recently Einstein, according to reports, has discovered a fourth dimension, perhaps even higher concepts. But such knowledge is too wonderful for me; it is high and I cannot attain unto it. Most of us will have to be content to live in and observe three dimensions till some new Euclid comes along to demonstrate how to get into the space-time continuum, whatever that is.)

The parallel to spiritual truth is here: Just as flat pictures lack the true fidelity of stereopticons, so until we experience Christian life in all three of its dimensions we know it only in part. As Paul expressed his hope to the Ephesians: "That you being rooted and grounded in love, may have power to comprehend with all the saints what is the breadth and length and height and depth, and to know the love of Christ, that you may be filled with all the fullness of God." What are these dimensions which bring fullness?

1. First there is the measurement of length. In our time we have seen an excessive emphasis upon individualism at the expense of community. In religion this has taken the form of focusing our attention almost wholly on our immediate, personal, individual encounter with God, and with the Church. We think of God primarily in terms of our own relations with Him here and now. This is all to the good as far as it goes—

by all means essential—but it fails to go far enough. It overlooks the whole historical character of our religion. There is a vast dimension of length to the Christian revelation, beginning with Abraham and continuing down to the present. We cannot comprehend the fullness of God's love until we see the long panorama of the centuries, until we recognize that we are part of a great tradition and ongoing community. Jesus himself regarded his own ministry in these terms. "I came not to destroy the law and the prophets but to fulfill them." He claimed a continuity with the long past.

We think too often of the Church in terms of its immediate aspect, what it is doing now and how it affects us. In papers written by young people of a confirmation class asked to tell why they thought the Church was important to the life of the world one answer appeared repeatedly: "The Church is important because it helps us defend ourselves against communism." The same answer would have come from a similar group of adults. Unconsciously we judge the Church in terms of how it serves some immediate world crisis. Again, this is quite legitimate, for unless the Church speaks some clear word to man in crisis it ceases to be the Church. True, the Church may be a defense against communism. But that is quite incidental; you might also speak truly of the Church as a defense against capitalism. The main business of the Church is to proclaim the majesty, the judgment, the mercy, and the love of God in Jesus Christ, in this crisis and in all crises.

So one thing the dimension of length gives us is a truer perspective on our faith and on ourselves. It saves us from the partial perspective of judging all things by the immediate effect, liberating us from being prisoners of the moment.

With no experience, no recognition, no appreciation of three thousand years of revelation in the community of the faithful, how could we have any true perspective. Obviously we cannot live over again three thousand years of history. But we can through study, meditation, and spiritual communion strive to capture at least a little of the sense of an ongoing community with acquired traditions and a glorious fellowship across the centuries. We must be aware of the long heritage of the years, of the experiences other men have had with God, of how God has judged the works and lives of former nations and people, of the truths and insights which our fathers and forefathers gained through their struggles. So many times in the past decade and more we have heard people asking in deep perplexity, What on earth is God doing now? Why does God allow war to continue unbroken? What does all this suffering mean if God is truly our loving Father? We do not know the answer to these questions, but we come nearer to understanding if we know that past generations have asked them too. It brings the consolation of strength to know that other men have found help in facing them and living with them, and that men do find redemption *through* suffering. But this kind of understanding does not appear to anyone's mind overnight. It is part of the legacy of our Christian history.

Still further, the dimension of length gives us great resources of a heritage to draw upon. One of the discoveries of our generation has been that the people who stood up to evil with strength and made the most stirring witness for truth have been the people who drew upon their heritage of faith. They have not been the rugged individualists who tried to stand free of all traditions and communities. "We have reached the point," observes Reinhold Niebuhr, "where the more traditional and historic churches, with their theological discipline, are more successful in evoking a genuinely Christian faith than the churches which dispensed with these disciplines. American Protestantism cannot regain its spiritual vitality without seeking a better synthesis between religious spontaneity and religious tradition and discipline." [1] We know in our thoughtful moments that to recall what has gone by acts as a moral stimulus. Sacred memories coming down the length of days serve to remind us of standards which we have inherited and to which some fresh loyalty is owed. James Moffatt once expressed these truths in provocative sentences:

> Whether the issue is religious or political, the saving of the sane is to be conscious that spirits in a hurry, who ignore the nexus between "then" and "now" do so at their own peril. . . . Except in the case of scientific discoveries, little good is done to the great world upon the whole by notions that were never heard of until this morning. Short and easy ways of effecting a change or reform are apt to end in long trouble for the next generation. Hasty improvisations which in lordly fashion dispense with experience have an awkward way of tripping up those who are at their beck and call.[2]

So Christian faith has its long horizontal dimension of length across the centuries. Out of this measure come patience, mature wisdom, discipline, and the faith of finding God in history.

2. The full Christian life has also the measurement of breadth. Christianity is as wide as it is long. In fact it is easy to emphasize length of tradition at the expense of breadth of outreach. Churches that are long on tradition may be short on world-wide concern. So the dimension of breadth gives

needed support to the long measurement. Much capital has been made out of the Boston clergyman of whom it was said that he believed in the Fatherhood of God, the brotherhood of man, and the neighborhood of Boston. Perhaps this humor derives from the fact this describes most of us with more truth than we care to concede. Look at it again in terms of the techniques of three-dimensional moving pictures. One of the approaches to "movies in depth" is to use a wide curved screen in order to create peripheral extension of vision. Peripheral vision is what is seen out of a normal pair of eyes looking straight ahead. Normal is 180 degrees, half a circle. The familiar movie screen in regular theaters showing the conventional type of picture has a field of about thirty degrees. There are many people who profess to be Christian whose field of spiritual vision is limited to about thirty degrees—no focusing ever upon life that lies outside that limited arc of vision. One of the sins that so easily besets us is that our spiritual focus is so restricted: our own church, part of our own city, a narrow range of associations, a few aspects of our own denomination. Against anything beyond these we wear blinders.

By contrast, in the showing of some types of three-dimensional pictures there is a curved screen that provides a field of vision of about 142 degrees. It seems to wrap itself around the audience and create the illusion that the viewer is actually "in" the picture. That is precisely what the dimension of breadth does in our Christian faith. *It wraps itself around the whole world of men and makes them seem to be "in" God's picture!* The illusion of the movie screen is a symbol of the reality in religion. Jesus saw the world in its full width: "Go therefore and make disciples of all." Until we feel God's concern for all men we really don't know God at all.

Once I lived for about a week in the home of a country doctor in northern Vermont. We had known this man as a summer family doctor; we loved him as one of the rare spirits in our circle of friends quite aside from our unbounded professional respect for the many healings he had helped bring to us. But we knew him only from office calls or personal visits to our summer camp in times of sickness. It was a we-to-him relationship. Then I lived with him for a week and saw the wonderful breadth of his practice. I drove with him on a day's calls—far up into the hills to check on a confinement case, into dilapidated farmhouses to bind up injured bodies, into homes where children lay feverish with pain, to a farm where he did all he could to ease the troubles of a blind lady. A whole valley of people, people of whom I had been totally unaware although I had summered nearby for ten years, "belonged" to him. And he belonged to them! As we sat one evening in his study after the last patient had gone from the office I looked at this man whom I thought I had known for years, and realized I was seeing him for the first time because I understood at last the width of his life and the breadth of his spirit.

Many have made the same discovery about God. When they have been called out of the confining neighborhood of narrow interests into a quickening touch of a world-wide fellowship of God's children they have sensed for the first time the breadth of Christ's love. People living in the world's valley of troubles of whom we knew nothing we discover to be children of the same God and Father who comes to our calls and heals our sins and sorrows. Our God is a great God, but you don't know Him till you see Him loving His whole family, black, white, red, brown, and yellow. In the Catskill Mountains back of Kingston, New York, is a road that winds along a hillside bordering an exquisitely lovely lake. Near a place where many stop to drink in the beauty of this scene with its cool breath of forest and sky is a sign: Ashokan Reservoir—New York City Water Supply. Your mind makes the journey of ninety miles to the south and you realize that the real business of this lake is not to provide anyone's private aesthetic enjoyment. It is to quench the thirst and cleanse the stain of a whole city of men. Here is a reservoir flowing down from majestic mountains through a long aqueduct and out into millions of blighted homes and lives with refreshment, cleansing, and new life. So it is with God's love. Though it is wonderful to behold it, rejuvenating to commune with Him in the mountaintops of fellowship, we do not really know His reservoir of love until we see it flowing out to a whole world thirsty for the water of eternal life, stained with sin and needing to be washed. To the sinkholes of iniquity in our great cities, to the compounds of despair where humanity huddles in fear across Asia and Africa, to the places where men devise evil against their fellows in lands of totalitarian bondage, to the brokenhearted who cry in the long night watches—this is where the reservoir of God's love drains. This is the breadth of Christian faith and life. Out of this dimension come compassion, release from the loneliness of separation, the faith of finding God in a world-wide community of men.

3. The third dimension in our Christian life is the measurement of height and depth. Life is not all lived on the horizontal plane of length and breadth; there are heights and

depths in human experience where the soul leaps up to touch Reality above and beyond human life. We likewise discover abysmal depths beneath ourselves. For some people, notably the mystics, this is the first dimension of their religion. They are immediately persuaded of God's presence and are able to rise above all earthly entanglements to commune with Him. Other folk find this the last and hardest dimension to know. They cry with Job, "Oh, that I knew where I might find Him." And yet, the vertical dimension is there; within us we feel a strange impulse to fling our souls upward toward the height. We surmise that life is not complete with mere time and space.

When men have flung their souls out upon the winds they have found God. Yea, better yet, God has found them. Jesus promised both of these gifts in the third dimension. "The Father will give you the Holy Spirit to be with you forever, for he dwells with you and will be in you. . . . In me you may have peace."

The experience of the race confirms this. Souls of great stature bear the report to us of an upward dimension that does not end in futility, of a personal "I–Thou" encounter with God by which life is supported. In 1832 John Henry Newman journeyed to the Mediterranean in great anguish of spirit. He did not know where his life was leading or how to find his way through the turbulence of unanswered questions. Yet he prayed:

> Lead kindly light, amid the encircling gloom,
> Lead thou me on;
> The night is dark, and I am far from home,
> Lead thou me on.
> Keep thou my feet; I do not ask to see the distant scene,
> One step enough for me.

Newman was sustained by the overarching love of God, and while he did not come into the light where many of us might come, it was to the same God and Father of us all to whom he could pray with confidence at the end, even as you and I: "O Lord, support us all the day long, until the shadows lengthen, and the evening comes, and the busy world is hushed, and the fever of life is over, and our work is done. Then grant us a safe lodging and a holy rest and peace at the last."

Our own personal experience confirms this. In moments of great joy or fathomless sorrow we feel the touch or pull of Someone or something utterly beyond ourselves, giving inward assurance that life has a dimension not measured in length or width.

Most of all Jesus Christ himself confirms the third dimension. On the Mount of Transfiguration, at Calvary, and in the Resurrection we see life lifted up unto the very presence of God. These are but the shining summits of an experience that was Christ's and can be ours every day. Without this dimension of personal encounter the other dimensions lose all their meaning, for length becomes merely a treadmill of centuries, and breadth means only a family grown too large for the house in which we dwell. But see these things in the third dimension and their everlasting meaning stands clear.

On the other hand, what about the dimension of depth? The Christian faith is altogether realistic about the profound depths in the human soul as well as the heights. Faith sees the awful evil of life as being not somewhere outside of us, or somewhere behind us in history or in our biological ancestry, but somewhere beneath us, buried in the soul of every person. And faith knows that not by education or science or kindly human good will, important as all of these may be, can this evil ever be brought to bondage. Who is going to save man from himself? There are great depths beneath us into which we shall certainly fall if we are left to our own devices. Only by a transcendent love from beyond ourselves can we ever be saved from ourselves. This is the gift of the gospel.

Mebane Ramsey gives us in a picture the truth about the depths and our hope in the third dimension. A group of visitors was being shown through the Carlsbad Caverns in New Mexico. In the group were a little man of eleven years of age and his seven-year-old sister. When they came to the deepest point in the caves the lights were turned out. So great was the darkness in the depths of the earth that the little girl began to cry. Bravely the boy put his arm around the shoulders of his young sister and reassured her saying, "Don't you cry. There's a man here who knows how to turn the lights on."

That is the good news of God for the deepest dimension of our lives, One who has turned on the light which no darkness can put out.

13

A Sight to Make Hell Tremble

The Communion and Fellowship of the Church

For where two or three are gathered together in my name, there am I in the midst of them.—Matthew 18:20

Now to him who by the power at work within us is able to do far more abundantly than all that we ask or think, to him be glory in the church and in Christ Jesus to all generations, for ever and ever. Amen.
—Ephesians 3:20–21

IN C. S. Lewis' *Screwtape Letters* the Devil in hell is giving advice to one of his agents on the earth assigned to keep a man from becoming a real Christian. The intended victim has joined the church and has the Devil's agent worried. But Screwtape gives this assurance: "There is no need to despair" (if the victim does not see the Church itself) "as we see her spread out through all time and space and rooted in eternity, terrible as an army with banners. That, I confess, is a spectacle which makes our boldest tempters uneasy." [1] It is hard to imagine truer words put into more vivid picture: the Christian Church with all her banners flying striking fear into the heart of hell. To define hell may be a task for theologians and philosophers, but who of us cannot describe it? We live in the midst of hell. At one point Sir Thomas Browne wrote, "The heart of man is the place the Devil dwells in; I feel sometimes a hell within myself." We see a world in hell and we know the Devil within our own souls. For something that can cause this kingdom of evil to tremble no wonder the seer of old cried "Hallelujah!"

If God be for us we should expect that He would give us an instrument of divine power in whose force we can stand and move against the kingdoms of this world. The Church is that instrument! It is in terms of a power against evil, of God thrusting Himself into the kingdoms of this world that we ought to think of the Church here. Theologically speaking the Church is the "body of Christ." One trouble, however, is that not many of us speak the technical language of theology—and among those who do the "body of Christ" has too often remained a mystical and static notion. Actually the "body of Christ" is a dynamic living creation, altogether committed in the struggle between heaven and hell. The Church is certainly one of the great mysteries of which we are stewards, broader and deeper than the farthest reaches of our minds, not to be encompassed by one sermon or any sermons. But we can move toward the truth if we think of it as God's gift for our warfare.

We can construct a sufficiently accurate map of hell by looking at it from four directions and then see how the Church with all her banners flying is a sight to make hell tremble. (1) We can define hell first of all as the enemy-occupied territory of sin, the kingdom of the soul and the kingdoms of this world where sin holds us in its grip. (2) Again, hell is the condition of our separation from each other. We live together in crowds but our lives are unrelated. We are alone, sometimes even in the most intimate relationships and at the hours of great crisis. Alone and lonely—we are in hell. (3) Hell is also the prison house of time and space where the soul never breaks free of the confines of the immediate and the temporal. (4) Finally, hell is a life that is lived with no destination in heaven. To shake these kingdoms of sin, separation, bondage to the perishables of time, and death God has given us the Church. Let us consider the way.

1. Dibelius has described Christ's coming to earth as an advance into enemy-occupied territory. It is as though God knew He could not conquer evil and destroy sin's power except as He came Himself into the kingdom where sin rules, defeating it on its own ground. Recall that picture that shocked a whole nation in the early days of our struggle for the islands of the Pacific in World War II. It was a picture of an American soldier lying face down, dead, at the water's edge of a Pacific island. In that one figure was gathered up the whole meaning of the cost of conquest of those islands. This was the price of advance into enemy-occupied territory, for our sakes. The price was paid; the territory was won and it was "ours." The cross, which the Church holds at its center, is the reminder of the price paid by Christ that the territory of sin might be ours. Christ came into the realms of life where sin held men in its grip, conquered sin by destroying its power, and defeated even our last enemy death by his Resurrection. The Church is the living power of the Resurrection, for the power that conquered sin and death is alive at the heart of the Church, the power of the risen Christ. The "enemy" still occupies the territory where we live. But if this Resurrection power lives on in the life of the Church, and if the Church becomes a real Resurrection society, then hell has reason to tremble. For here is a force adequate to hold back the tide of evil and dethrone its ruling sway. It is power that was won at a supreme price. The Church, with a crucified and

risen Lord at her heart, is witness to both the price and the power.

People who are living in the power of that victory are new people—and the place you find that power to be reborn is in the fellowship of the Church. In the Resurrection Jesus came to his disciples making them new creatures, one by one—Peter, Thomas, the two at Emmaus. But it was in a fellowship that the power took hold at Pentecost and in Rome. And it is through the communion of Christ in his Church that the power takes hold of us.

A friend writes from Oxford University of the strange feeling in the Oxford colleges to walk up the stairways whose treads have been worn into little hollows by the passage of many feet. One thinks of all the famous feet that have climbed the stairs of Oxford; it is a great thing to follow in those steps. But one thinks even more of the famous feet that have climbed the steps of the Church and found here a new life in the continuing power of the Resurrection. We walk where they walked. H. R. L. "Dick" Sheppard was once showing a group of visitors through Canterbury Cathedral. When they came to those famous chancel steps, the destination of so many thousands of pilgrim journeys, Sheppard took one man and pressed his knee to the step saying, "Kneel here; it is a great thing to kneel where faithful pilgrims have knelt in days ahead of you." We do that in the communion of the Church. We kneel where others have knelt and then risen to go out victors over the destructive power of alcohol, sex, temper, hate, weakness, fear because they found at the heart of the Church One in whose grip they could handle these things. The Church is the company of faithful where this power lives. It is a great thing to walk where they walked, kneel where they bowed. You may find this power somewhere outside the Church. But it always comes as the overflow *from* the Church, a legacy received *through* the Church, and unless it leads back *into* the Church and joins the body whence it came it shrivels and dies.

Now this power can die in the Church, too, where the Church becomes a country club, where it is just a reflection of the lives that come in through the doors. The Church has some miserable failures to its humiliation down through the years. True! But the failures have never destroyed the Resurrection power that mysteriously goes on from victory unto victory. And not only in personal affairs! That same mysterious power of the living Christ has nerved the Church for the heroic days of history: persecution in Rome, the costly challenge of the missionary advance, the campaigns against evils of slavery and exploitation, the stand of the confessional churches against Nazi idolatry when every other voice and witness faded out. In a company dwelling with Christ in their midst is a power that does not flinch before evil's towering assaults. Hell is afraid of that because that power cannot finally be defeated.

Here is the power of hell summed up in a few words. Gian-Carlo Menotti, the American composer, came up with this definition: "Hell begins on the day when God grants us a clear vision of all that we might have achieved, of all the gifts which we have wasted, of all that we might have done that we did not do. . . . For me the conception of hell lies in two words: 'too late.'" Peter and Judas looked into hell on the day of Calvary. Too late! But for Peter there was a Resurrection. At the heart of the Church is the proclamation of God's forgiveness. Those who receive it can be Peters,

They go through hell; they come out with new power. No wonder hell trembles at the sight of a Church whose flying banners have been raised by folk who were forgiven by the risen Christ. They know what hell is because they've been through it. But they know a stronger power.

2. Let's look at hell from another direction. A character in T. S. Eliot's *The Cocktail Party* says: "Hell is oneself. Hell is alone, the other figures in it merely projections. There is nothing to escape from and nothing to escape to. One is always alone." [2] Even simpler are the words of William Morris, "Fellowship is life, lack of fellowship is death; fellowship is heaven, and lack of fellowship is hell." Well, it is part of the strategy of the devil to keep people separated one from another, only superficially relating their lives to each other. The devil comes near succeeding in modern man's individualism. Life has become fractured, atomized. We are alone, our hearts can break, we can even die and the faceless "people" in the next apartment not even know, much less care. This is hell. Was it this that Matthew Arnold felt on *Dover Beach* in saying that the world

> Hath really neither joy, nor love, nor light,
> Nor certitude, nor peace, nor help for pain;
> And we are here as on a darkling plain
> Swept with confused alarms of struggle and flight,
> Where ignorant armies clash by night.

One person *alone* is no match for powerful armies, whether they be armies of entrenched evil or armies of the powers of darkness in our own souls. Even great masses of "separated" individuals are no match for the kingdoms of hell on the march. Ah, but suppose we broke down the walls between us, overcame our separation. Suppose somehow these atomized masses turned into people whose hearts and hands were joined in one communion, bound together by one spirit. Then hell had better tremble! Jesus said, "Where two or three are gathered together in my name"—which is to say, where two or three are gathered together in communion with one another in Christ's love—there will Christ be himself. This kind of communion shakes hell to its deepest pit because it drives the sword into the heart of despair. In a visible communion of people with Christ no one ever faces evil and sin alone. It is the alone-ness that yields us to despair, and despair is hell at its worst. But despair hath no dominion in communion.

Truth stands more clearly revealed on the far frontiers of life and death than in the murkiness of our daily life. Men who journey to these frontiers bear to us the report of truth we had not clearly seen. Such is the manner in which one of the great chapters of human adventure in our time illuminates our understanding of the Church. In 1950 the world was thrilled with the conquest of Annapurna, the first 26,000-foot peak to be climbed to its summit. Maurice Herzog and his companion, who reached the top, reflected on the moment:

> Our hearts overflowed with an unspeakable happiness. . . . If only the others could know. If only everyone could know. . . . My joy was touched with humility. It was not just one party that had climbed Annapurna today but a whole expedition. I thought of all the others in the camps perched on the slopes at our feet, and I knew it was because of their efforts and sacrifices that we had succeeded. . . . Together we knew toil, joy and pain. My fervent wish is that the nine of us who were united in the face of death should remain fraternally united through life.[3]

They were "one man." In their discovery of community in the face of death they had discovered the greatest secret of life. It was a communion fused together by the spirit of a great purpose. I think of that as an allegory for the Church: a whole community of people disciplined by a single loyalty and love, united in the face of death. Maurice Herzog wrote at the end of his book, "There are other Annapurnas in the lives of men": great summits to ascend, not in the Himalayas but towering above all the lowlands where we live. When you join a Christian fellowship you join a company which binds you to its heart, a company of those who walk with you now and those who have walked before. You no longer climb alone.

Think of this church, or any church of which you are a part. Others whose names you know, whose faces you love have broken trails ahead of you. Moreover, others in this very communion are loving you and climbing with you; they may not know all the hardships of your journey but they will belay you on the rope when the going is too steep for you alone. Still further, there are others in camps far down the slopes whom you have loved, who have labored for you and brought you up even this high. Their love is backing you up and still surrounds you now as you walk higher—a father, mother, life partner, child, friend. It is a great thing to climb in such a company. But it is more than a *company*. It is a *communion*. Herzog said that Annapurna bestowed its grace upon the climbers, the ideal blessed the men. Surely that is true of the Church. Christ bestows his grace upon the members, turning their association into communion.

A man once stood on the church steps watching a congregation assemble for worship. He knew most of them well. One by one they went up the steps and through the door, a pretty sorry bunch of folk, thought the man. Weak men and women, some of them spineless in character, others full of deceit. Get them all together and you've got a sad assembly! The whole is just as great as the sum of its parts. But then this man went into the church, joined the company in communion, felt the invisible "plus" element added to the sum of the whole. In Christ, this man discovered, the whole is greater than the sum of its parts. Communion exceeds the law of mathematics. As they stood to sing "My faith looks up to thee" the man was sure that something more than a company of frail men and women was in that room. In true communion is a lifting and delivering power that hell cannot bind.

3. Once more, hell is where people live with their eyes on the clock and on the ground, prisoners of time and space. It is good devilish strategy to keep a man's attention focused on petty annoyances, to make him behave as though he himself were a "clod of ailments," to lure him on into feverish activity, to keep him busy being busy. Then he will have no time to lift up his eyes unto the hills, no time to discover from whence his help comes. He will feel no need to touch the hem of God's garments, no desire to storm the gates of heaven. The devil wants men to think of this prison house of time and space as the true homeland of their souls. Then life can wither itself away, or wear itself out, with no transfusion of life from beyond itself, no blessing or benediction from above. Tramp the treadmill, eyes on the ground, until life goes out like a candle. This keeps life in hell.

But let a man see a church with banners flying—better still, let him enter that church and start to worship, to fling his soul upward to the heights—then hell is wise enough to know it's time to tremble. Men at worship are men in danger of discovering that the true homeland of their souls is not in the frantic round of busyness, that life is more than a clod of ailments, a cluster of annoyances, that life has dimensions neither clock nor calendar, looking glass nor yardstick can show. This is one great gift of Christ through the Church, the experience of pointing and lifting the soul toward God, above anxiety and away from fussiness. Dorothy Wordsworth once wrote in her Journal about Grasmere, her home in the Lake Country of England: "Very solemn in the last glimpse of twilight—it calls home the heart to quietness." That is a great ministry also of the Church. The elements of worship (a believing community, the familiar appointments of altar, cross, and candles, music, Bible, preaching)—all these call home the heart to quietness, to self-transcendence. To know that we are not prisoners of time and space is the gift of the Church at worship.

Ola Winslow writes of the early New Englanders and how they built their meetinghouses at the center of their villages, symbols of the vital center of life. This had a significance for the unconscious mind. "Somehow it embodied fundamental loyalties and created a state of mind in which these loyalties took on reality. . . . In some way it teased the thought of village men and women beyond village boundaries, and the Here and Now of their lives. It stood for the eternal against the transient."[4] If a man trusts himself to worship in spirit and in truth he finds his mind being teased beyond village boundaries, lured away from the Here and Now toward things eternal.

See in one lovely picture what worship does. Giordano Bruno, the Christian philosopher who was burned at the stake in 1600, grew up as a boy in the little town of Nola, twenty miles north of Naples. From Nola Mount Vesuvius looked like a great gray lifeless hill on the horizon. At the age of twelve Bruno went to Naples for the first time. When he stood on Vesuvius it turned out to be green and lovely, while Nola was gray and vague on the horizon. Bruno said, "Vesuvius was on my horizon. Now that I stand on it it isn't any longer the horizon; it is the center. There are other horizons beyond. If I could go and stand on them they in turn would be new centers." He wondered if that was the way the universe was constructed: every horizon was a new center. This led Bruno to the appalling hypothesis that the universe was infinite. Let a man make this discovery about life—that what seemed to be the dim, gray, distant horizons are actually lovely and green, that we can move from the center to the far horizon and make it a new center—let a man make this discovery and the whole of life will reflect the glow of this wonder. You can make that discovery when you join a company of believing, worshiping Christians. Worship can be a dreadful escape when we move to the far horizons of life and sit down and never come back. But worship can also be a way to the heart of God, which journey sends us back into life with new eyes. Nothing is safe after that journey, whether it be sin, prejudice, parochialism, sloth, pride. We have broken prison.

4. Our last view of hell is in a life with no destination beyond the grave. The devil has no fear of a church as long as it keeps its focus just on this life. The bigger the church, the busier, the more efficient, so much the better. In this the devil is smarter than the average church member. We say, "Let's not worry about heaven; we've no time or interest in a 'pie in the sky' religion, or all the obscurantism of otherworldliness. Let's make this the best of all possible worlds." This sounds modern, enlightened, emancipated. The devil

knows better. He knows that a Church seriously persuaded of its eternal destiny and the eternal life of all the souls in it is a terribly dangerous threat to be loose in the world. People whose citizenship is in a colony of heaven are people who regard their lives as expendable for righteousness' sake. Even death is swallowed up for people who are in communion with God, an indestructible communion in Christ. They "shine like stars in a dark world" and no darkness can put out their light. The source of their light is in the Church.

Many of the covenants in the early New England churches ended with the phrase, "as befits those whom God has bound together in a little bundle of eternal life." It may be a paradox beyond the grasp of the wisdom of this world, but people who live as befits those whom God has bound up in a little bundle of eternal life are fearsome adversaries for every evil thing in this world. Joseph Fort Newton once put it squarely on the line: "No promise is given to a Church that has suffered the forces of evil to give battle, a beleagured Church that apologizes for its gospel. Only to a Church militant against evil, storming the final fortress of wrong—for no other is a Church—shall be given the keys of the Kingdom; the power to open wide the gates of God to seeking, doubting, despairing men." It is in the tremendous conviction of the eternal destiny of life, found nowhere but in a Resurrection society, that a Church thinks it worthy to storm the final fortress of wrong.

Has this been too rosy a picture of the Church? Does the church you know fit it? Churches have often tragically chosen to specialize in irrelevancies, to lose the large aims in the minor technicalities. Churches can be "brigade minded," not "army minded." They can be the religious arm of the country club, the chamber of commerce, a political party at prayer. Stephen Spender's terrible indictment has been justified: "Religion stands, the Church blocking the sun." These charges are true. The Church stands accused; she pleads guilty, faces herself with shame. Jesus reserved his most severe wrath for the good people in "churches," religious hypocrites, guilty of the sins of the spirit. The Church at its best suffers this condemnation, more aware of her deepest sins than are her critics. But somewhere at her heart is One who promises still that where two or three are gathered together He will be there. So with whatever flaws, the Church is a little kingdom of love, an island in the seas of evil, joined by invisible bonds to a greater Kingdom beyond the horizon.

In the third century St. Cyprian wrote to a friend some words that still strike terror into hell:

> This seems a cheerful world, Donatus, when I view it from this fair garden, under the shadow of these vines. But if I climbed some great mountain and looked out over the wide lands, you know very well what I would see. Brigands on the high roads, pirates on the seas, in the amphitheaters men murdered to please the applauding crowds, under all roofs misery and selfishness. It is really a bad world, Donatus, an incredibly bad world. Yet in the midst of it I have found a quiet and holy people. They have discovered a joy which is a thousand times better than any pleasure of this sinful life. They are despised and persecuted, but they care not. They have overcome the world. These people, Donatus, are the Christians—and I am one of them.

It is this sight that shakes the Devil.

14

Found in the Stars

Assurance That Life Is Not Lost

For the Son of man came to save that which was lost.—Matthew 8:11 (marginal reading)

But now in Christ Jesus you who once were far off have been brought near in the blood of Christ.

—Ephesians 2:13

In all the descending circles of anxiety no fear more terrifies the heart of a man than the fear of being lost. Therefore no gift of the gospel brings greater joy than the good news: we are not lost! A Saviour has found us! This is the good news of Christmas. No wonder angels sang *gloria in excelsis*! Maxwell Anderson's *Lost in the Stars* is an adaptation for the musical theater of Alan Paton's *Cry, the Beloved Country*. It concerns people who not only were lost in a city but thought they were lost in the stars. This is a good place for a Christmas sermon to begin, for it was to little "lost" people that Christmas came.

At the close of the first act Stephen Kumalo, trying to hold together the pieces of his own shattered world, and surveying the awful darkness of tragedy, sin, fear, and death in the world of Johannesburg, sings this song:

> Before Lord God made the sea and the land
> He held all the stars in the palm of his hand,
> And they ran through his fingers like grains of sand,
> And one little star fell alone.

Then the Lord God hunted through the wide night air
For the little dark star on the wind down there—
And he stated and promised he'd take special care
So it wouldn't get lost again.

Now a man don't mind if the stars grow dim
And the clouds blow over and darken him,
So long as the Lord God's watching over them,
Keeping track how it all goes on.

But I've been walking through the night and the day
Till my eyes get weary and my head turns grey,
And sometimes it seems maybe God's gone away,
Forgetting the promise that we heard him say—
And we're lost out here in the stars—
Little stars, big stars,
Blowing through the night,
And we're lost out here in the stars.[1]

The voice of all mankind sings in those lines. Sometimes it seems that God's gone away. Later the poet catches the full fury of this fear as the Negro chorus sings:

Fear for the mines,
And for the prison,
And the cell from which there is no return?
Yes, we fear them,
Though we are many and they are few.

And the white chorus sings:

Who can lie peacefully abed
When the dark without window is troubled
By those who hate you for what you are and what you do?

And they join their fears in words that speak for men the world over:

Fear of the few for the many,
Fear of the many for the few.[2]

Symbolically, the stage directions following this chorus read simply: *The lights go out.* They have gone out in fear-haunted lives, lost in the stars. Is there no answering call, and no rescue?

Christmas is the answer. As Anderson put it in one of his finest choruses:

> Each lives alone
> In a world of dark,
> Crossing the skies in a lonely arc,
> Save when love leaps out like a leaping spark
> Over thousands, thousands of miles! [3]

Save when love leaps out like a leaping spark! That describes Christmas—God's love leaping out of the darkness like a long-awaited comet from out of the void. And across all the thousands and thousands of miles of earth, and the thousands of years of time, that leaping spark has kindled a great light for the people who walked in darkness. Christ's coming finds men lost and wandering in the valleys of despair. It brings them three gifts: an announcement, an invitation, and a promise.

1. First, Christmas is the announcement that we have been found in the stars. This is the good news that shall be to all people for all time. God's entry into the world in the person of Jesus Christ is the affirmation that the affairs of this planet are not matters of indifference to God. Not only does He know where it is, but He cares about each person on it. The joy of Christmas is at least in part the joy of discovering that our insignificant lives have meaning to God. Therefore they take on a new significance to us and to each other. God thinks of New Haven, not as a place where one hundred and sixty thousand people live, but as a place where you live and I live, where we work, and play, and love, and have our being.

God counts us not as a mob but as individuals—everyone, his name and his soul, known by God to the farthest limits of space-time and on into eternity. This is what is the matter with an economic system that counts people by what they can bring in a production plan. It sabotages a greater Plan that has priority over all economic plans. Not just because it is humanly degrading, although that in itself is sufficient sanction, but because it wantonly throws away a commodity (the soul of a person) for which God has paid the ultimate price to find. That is what is the matter with a social system that casts out its minorities (and even sometimes its racial majorities!). To discard human lives is obscene from the human perspective; against God it is the cardinal transgression for it flouts the heart and soul of His purpose in "finding" the souls of men. Edwin Markham has gathered this truth up in lines of provocative verse:

> Now have the homely things been made
> Sacred, and a glory on them laid,
> Now that the King has gone this way,
> Great are the things of every day! [4]

The homely things that are the stuff of every day become holy things in new dimension since Christ hallowed them by his uncommon touch.

Halfway between the vernacular and the profane is a much used expression—the superlative form of the word evil: *God-forsaken.* We speak of somewhere as a God-forsaken place, some job as God-forsaken work, some dwelling as a God-forsaken home. You can't go any lower than that. *Christ Stopped at Eboli* is the title of a novel centering in an Italian town which according to legend Christ did not enter. Were there such a town it would in very truth be hell. But then

God's love leaps out again like a leaping spark over all the deserts and Ebolis where we imagined He had forsaken us and lost us saying, "No! Your life matters. The life of your child matters. And your friend. And the commonest life of all. On all these have I laid a glory, for the uncommonest life of earth and heaven has consecrated the common to be uncommon, the ordinary to be extraordinary, the insignificant to be eternal."

Howard Thurman tells of talking with a young German woman who had escaped from the Nazis.[5] She described the effect Hitler had on the German youth, the youth who had lost their sense of belonging. "They did not count; there was no center of hope for their marginal egos. Hitler told them: 'No one loves you—I love you; no one will give you work—I will give you work; no one wants you—I want you.' And when they saw the sunlight in his eyes they dropped their tools and followed him." What tragedy that German youth had to find their lives in Hitler. But seeing what happened, can you doubt the power that comes from "being found"? Christmas is the celebration of this same discovery in the redeeming announcement of God saying, "I love you—I will give you work—I want you." And when we see the sunlight in the face of Christ, with all confidence we can drop the primitive tools with which we have been trying to scratch the surface of life's meaning, and follow him. As Paul put it to the Gentiles—and who of us is not a Gentile where these things are concerned?—"But now in Christ Jesus you who were once far off have been brought near!"

2. This leads us directly to the second celebration of Christmas. The birth of Christ goes beyond a mere announcement—the announcement of even so great a piece of news as God's

finding us—to become an invitation. God's is the invitation to become His sons. Christmas doesn't end like a game of hide-and-seek, with all the players scattering to their previous interests. It's not just "lost and found" we're playing, as though God, or someone less than God, were to exclaim: "Oh yes, I see it. Over there in the Milky Way near the sun. That's the place!" and then go on to other pursuits. This is a divine pursuit, but it's a case of "finders keepers." God "found" us through Christ because He wanted us to be His forever. To show us that our home is not an everlasting spiritual void God Himself became flesh with our flesh, spirit with our spirit.

> Born to raise the sons of earth,
> Born to give them second birth.

That's what Christmas means, if you had to say it in two lines.

As C. S. Lewis has put it so memorably: "God became man to turn creatures into sons; not simply to produce better men of the old kind but to produce a new kind of man." God wants *us* to be new creatures. Why otherwise did His love leap out across thousands of miles of earth and thousands of years of time to find us? As Lewis again suggests, we often behave as though the gospel and its gifts were primarily for someone else, "the little, low, timid, warped, thin-blooded, lonely people, or the passionate, sensual, unbalanced people." Whenever we find ourselves thinking this way it would be a good thing if we remembered that "nice" people get lost too. We can be lost in all the old familiar ways, lost in pride, in self-satisfaction, in greed, in anger, in lust. As one commentator said of the lost sheep in Jesus' parable, "we nibble ourselves lost." Perhaps until God finds us we don't even know we're lost, so closely have we been intent upon cropping away at the green grass of our own satisfactions. Getting along pretty well, too, thank you, with life worked out in slick style. Lots of good friends, plenty of activities to take up time and energy, here and there a "favorite charity," a good church, a fine school. Who could ask for more? And then all of a sudden something unlooked for happens. A great light shines *for us,* in the radiance of which lesser lights grow pale, even as the morning star dims before the rising sun. We go out into the night and find a light coming down *upon us.* Morning stars sing together *for us.* In a great love we fulfill ourselves and the face of all the world is changed. In pursuit of some high ideal we find our freedom and win our souls. In some burning fire of forgiveness, or some tragic encounter with sin, or some consuming visitation of sorrow we feel our hearts strangely warmed by an upholding of a love transcending all our own endeavors. We wake to the discovery that *we* were lost, too, wandering about in jungles or pastures of pleasure and self-enclosed satisfactions. In the light of the Christmas star all things become new. How else can we take this but that God wants us for something better than we were?

The Magi in T. S. Eliot's poem "The Journey of the Magi" speak of how this happened to them.

> There was a Birth, certainly,
> We had evidence and no doubt. I had seen birth and death,
> But had thought they were different; this Birth was
> Hard and bitter agony for us, like Death, our death.
> We returned to our places, these Kingdoms,
> But no longer at ease here, in the old dispensation.
> With an alien people clutching their gods.
> I should be glad of another death.[6]

That's what Bethlehem does to life. The old dispensation that once seemed so full now seems so empty. It's not so simple a thing, going to the manger, adoring the Madonna and Child, and then hurrying on to some other engagement. It's all right if we can just sit it out somewhere and watch the star, wise men, and shepherds, as we might watch a church nativity pageant from the balcony. But we find if we really go to Bethlehem nothing is likely to be the same again. It turns out to be not enough, going back to doctor up the old life a bit. We want to begin a glorious new life. There is more than one meaning in the fact that the Magi returned to their own country by *another* way. Having knelt at the feet of the Christ child the old way was no longer good enough. Christmas is an invitation to follow the Christ into a new way of loving each other, a new way of caring for our children, a new way of transacting the affairs of market and mine, a new way in the affairs of nations, a new way of living and a new way of dying.

Not long ago two British astronomers detected intensive radio emanations from the point in the northern constellation of Cassiopeia where one of the three supernova known to man in the Milky Way galaxy—Tycho's Star—flamed in November, 1572. According to the announcement of these scientists, "There is no visible object in the neighborhood of the heavens where this star was observed by the old astronomer Tycho Brahe, but, the new observations show, there must be left there something extremely hot. It is a powerful source of radiation." Though the star has been invisible for nearly four hundred years, the radiation is still reaching the earth. The Star of Bethlehem, whatever it may have been in the astronomical configurations, sent out a message through the skies which has been reaching the earth ever since. Although the visible image of the star has long since faded, the divine radio impulses are still coming. God wants us still, to be His sons. That is a powerful source of radiation.

3. But if Christmas is the announcement that we have been found, and the invitation to follow the Christ until he makes us sons of God it is above all God's promise to those who follow Him in love to lead them home. John Erskine has a provocative poem of Christmas called "Kings and Stars" the last verse of which tells us:

> The world widens by starlight
> The mind reaches,
> Stars beget journeys.[7]

Stars do beget journeys; from the beginning men have followed the stars across trackless seas and unknown wilds. The journey which the Star of Bethlehem begets is the journey with Christ to our home, our home in God. Home is not a place but a partnership, not so much a residence as a relationship. A family takes its home with them wherever they go. A father, mother, and children who are joined together by ties stronger than life itself will be "at home" whether in Kalamazoo or the Klondike, Timbuktu or Texas. After the same fashion, when we dwell day after day with our heavenly Father, we are at home. When we lose that relationship, no matter that we dwell in marble halls, we wander restlessly. For life without any ultimate reference, eternal destiny, transcending purpose is not life at all, for it is written, "Man shall not live by bread alone, but by every word that proceedeth out of the mouth of God."

A nation can be homeless when it loses its relationship to a divine ordination, or it can be at home when it ties in "a living tether, the priest and prince and thrall," and "lifts a single sword" of devotion to the Creator and Sustainer of all nations. For "it is God who has made of one blood all nations of men and established the bounds of their habitation."

A church can be homeless, even though it be named a Church of the Redeemer or Christ Church, if through all aspects of its life there is no evidence of a shared partnership with God. Or a church can be "at home" in whatever material circumstances, if its greatest and least endeavors are toward a divine purpose. Stars beget journeys, and the greatest one of all is to our home.

But it is His star we must follow, wherever it leads, even when other stars seem to promise more and shine with brighter blaze. December has two birthdays: on December 10, 1942, man first discovered the process of nuclear fission in a little room beneath the Chicago Stadium; on December 25 we celebrate the birthday of Jesus Christ. Out of the discovery made at the birth which came within our lifetime man has brought the secret of the stars down to earth. As the *New York Times* pointed out editorial-wise: "Man used to wonder why the stars shine. Now he knows. He even knows how to create a little ephemeral star on earth. But he does not yet know whether this star is to light the doom of all his culture, all his hopes and all his civilization." We know how to build hydrogen into helium now, the process that lights the stars in the heavens. We have literally brought the stars down to earth and in so doing we have sought to rival God. But in those stars lighted by our own hands we can only be lost forever. The real saving secret of the stars came down to earth, not to the Chicago Stadium, but two thousand years ago to a manger in

Bethlehem. We've always faced this terrible choice, from Eden to Eniwetok, but we face it now with a terrible clarity: to journey *onward* and perish in the radiation of our man-made stars, or to journey *homeward* in the radiation of God's love in Christ. Or to put the issue more squarely in the term of judgment where we face it: the hydrogen-helium fusion can only be redeemed by a mightier fusion, the fusion of God's Spirit with our own, in the released energy of which He promises—

> To an open house in the evening
> Home shall men come,
> To an older place than Eden
> And a taller town that Rome.
> To the end of the way of the wandering star,
> To the things that cannot be and that are,
> To the place where God was homeless
> And all men are at home.[8]

15

Beyond the Last Page

New Life Beyond Our Last Page

But there are also many other things which Jesus did; were every one of them to be written, I suppose that the world itself could not contain the books that would be written.—John 21:25

My brothers, I do not consider myself to have fully grasped even now that purpose for which Christ grasped me. But I do concentrate on this: I leave the past behind and with hands outstretched to whatever lies ahead I go straight for the goal—my reward the honour of being called by God in Christ.—Phillippians 3:13, 14 (J. B. Phillips, *Letters to Young Churches*)

We come now to the Great Divide, the highest Summit in the mountain ranges of faith, the place where the ways divide at the peak which most distinguishes our gospel and its gifts: the word and promise of new life beyond the last page of life that we can read. Whether that last page be the report of sin, loneliness, failure, frustration, or death, the supreme gift of the gospel is a word of hope for pages to come. Consider the parallel in the world of books. How often have you read a book that ended just where you wanted the story to go on! Just as new horizons began to open, the story ends leaving you in wonder about what happened at those horizons. Or with great decisions still to be made the author rings down the curtain. Or with decisive questions yet unanswered we are left only to guess at the course of events. Sometimes this happens because the author himself never finishes the work, sometimes because the action shifted to some new plane where the author chose not to follow, sometimes because the next events passed beyond the author's sight and knowledge.

Robert Louis Stevenson died while writing what might have been his greatest book, *The Weir of Hermiston.* At the point where the book ends a dark shadow has fallen over the love between Archie and Christina: a shadow which Archie cannot understand but for which he in some way feels responsible. These are the last two sentences:

"In vain he looked back over the interview; he saw not where he had offended. It seemed unprovoked, a wilful convulsion of brute nature. . . ." Stevenson died before he could tell us more. What happened beyond that last page?

One of the greatest novels ever written, Dostoevski's *Crime and Punishment,* leaves us with the same longing to go further. Raskolnikov has finally repented for a crime which he committed. He has found peace and won the love of Sonia. But he must expiate this crime by seven years of exile in Siberia. This is Dostoevski's ending:

> Seven years, only seven years! At the beginning of their happiness, at certain moments, they were both ready to look upon those seven years as so many days. He did not even realize that the new life was not given him for nothing, that he would have to pay a great price for it, that he would have to pay for it by a great act of heroism in the future.
>
> But that is the beginning of a new story, the story of the gradual rebirth of a man, the story of his gradual regeneration, of his gradual passing from one world to another. That might be the subject of a new story. Our present story is ended.

What was that great act of heroism to be? We wish we could go on and live with these people in their new life. We cannot go beyond the last page.

In 1924 George Mallory and Andrew Irvine attempted to reach the summit of Mount Everest. Watching their last assault on the 29,000-foot peak one of the party who remained at the highest bivouac, 27,000 feet, described it in these words

> At about half-past twelve there was a sudden clearing of the atmosphere; and the entire summit of Everest was unveiled. A belt of driving mist sweeping across the northern face failed to reach as far as the summit and left the final pyramid standing out clear against the blue sky. Suddenly I noticed high up in the almost perpendicular wilderness a moving black speck. And then I saw another speck move up to join the first. They seemed to be going strong. Then the mist swept up and the whole fascinating vision vanished.

That was the last that was ever seen of those men. Did Mount Everest kill them in revenge after they had attained the victory? Who knows? The two men who reached the summit twenty-nine years later found no clue. Mount Everest holds the secret beyond the last page of human sight.

One of the most famous stories with a tantalizing ending is Frank Stockton's "The Lady or the Tiger." A youth so bold as to love the king's daughter is condemned to open one of two doors. Behind one is a fascinating girl whom he must marry, behind the other a tiger. The king's daughter learns the secret and signals her lover to open one of the two doors—but which? That's where the story ends.

Books are full of last pages that beckon our imagination onward into unknowns. So is life. There is in the Bible a book that ends just where we most wish it would continue. The Gospel of John ends with this sentence: "There are also many other things which Jesus did; were every one of them to be written the world could not contain the books." What things? How we would like to know some of the other things Jesus did! The Evangelist leaves us just at the summit of the highest peak in all man's history. What lies beyond? What did Jesus do in the realms beyond the horizons of the four Gospels? We don't know them all. John spoke the truth indeed when he said, "The world itself could not contain the books to tell all that has happened." But we are reading here a book written barely seventy-five or eighty years after the Resurrection. We have nineteen hundred years of advantage over John. *We do know many of the things that have happened beyond that last page.* Only God knows them all. But generation after generation have added their pages to the gospel. Where John's Gospel ends the gospel of what Christ has done in history begins. And beyond the last page of every written record is the gospel of what Christ has done for you and for me. No one will ever add pages to Stevenson or Dostoevski, at least not the pages the authors would have added. But Christ has added pages to the gospel for life. Let us look at some of them, for they are the earnest of what may be added beyond your last page.

1. There could be millions of pages added to tell of Christ's victory over sin. Ford Maddox Ford wrote a book in 1926 called *A Man Could Stand Up*. The title refers to one of the overwhelming effects which the Armistice of World War I had on the men in the trenches, a psychological effect as well as physical. After years of crouching in the trenches, now at last they could stand up without fear of being mowed down by machine-gun fire. What a tremendous day when a man could stand up free of fear! Transfer that idea to the spiritual and emotional life and you have a description of one colossal effect of the Resurrection of Jesus Christ. In his power and by his grace men have found in the risen Christ a power great

enough to pick their soiled lives up out of the trenches of evil and set them on their feet. On this Easter anniversary now are men and women who on other Easters were crouching down in deep trenches of sinful attitudes, crippling habits, paralyzing fears. Today they stand and sing, "Christ the Lord is risen today! Alleluia!" They sing it with glad conviction because the great love of God put them on their feet again. They have found in Christ the confirmation of a power greater than themselves who could pick them up.

Peter could add one such page. After a miserable failure—cowardice, dishonesty, betrayal—in the power of the risen Lord he stood up out of the trench and became the Rock. Christ has given men both the desire and the ability to stand up out of trenches of selfishness, trenches of drunkenness, trenches of weakness. What has he not done for people who were slaves to their emotions, their environment, slaves to all evil influence? William Lyon Phelps once commented, "There are some people who are all right at three o'clock in the afternoon, but watch out for them at three o'clock in the morning. They are all right in Yonkers but look out for them in Paris. They are all right when they associate with virtuous people but look out for them when they associate with evil companions." True enough; they are people who are weak at the center, at the mercy of every time and place. Then Christ takes hold and they become dependable as a rock, any time, any place, in any company. What glorious pages these would all be if we could read them.

2. Then there could be volumes, whole libraries, added to the gospel telling of Christ's victory over defeat. In the Yale libraries are nearly four million volumes. But the Yale libraries are not large enough to include all that could be written of

how Jesus turned defeat into victory. The minister of one of our large and influential churches tells this story of a man who came to him seemingly whipped by life. With this man the game had gone to the ninth inning and he was being badly beaten, both by flaws in his own character (thus giving the affair the element of genuine tragedy) and by circumstances that caught him as helpless victim. His wife had left him to run off with another man, his job had lost all of its challenge and appeal so that he was now failing and close to receiving a pink slip in his pay envelope. The man was attracted to the church by a sermon subject, "How Christ Can Deal with Your Problem." Having no confidence that anything would happen he went anyway because the alternative seemed to be nothing, or even death itself. Just enough of a spark of hope was kindled in that service to bring the man back to see the minister in person. They talked for two hours. The minister talked about the love of God that was equal even to the staggering defeat of the cross. After a while the man was suddenly seized as by a new hope. He said to the minister, "I don't know what it is but there must be something there. If God could do that for Jesus He could do it for me, couldn't He? I want it. I need it!"

The preacher answered him without the slightest hesitation. "He not only could, but He will!" They prayed about it. The man walked out a new person. He had still his problem; his wife had not returned, and he would need to seek a new job. But he was a new man inside.

Toward the close of his life even one so close to God as Paul came to pages beyond which he could not read. "I do not consider myself to have fully grasped that purpose for which Christ grasped me. But I leave the past behind and with hands outstretched to whatever lies ahead go straight for the goal." Paul found glorious new pages beyond his last page of mystery—"Henceforth there is laid up for me a crown of righteousness"—and so did the beaten young man.

Robert Louis Stevenson was a man up against it. Overwhelmed by disaster and adversity, yet in his religious faith he won through so that he could one day write: "I believe in an ultimate decency of things; ay, and if I woke in hell I should still believe it." Christ does stoop to rescue us in defeat and adversity. Thanks be to God who giveth us the victory!

3. Other whole libraries can be added beyond the last page of our Bible gospel because of what people have done who saw the world anew through the eyes of Christ. A few years ago a woman in Brooklyn bequeathed her eyes to the eye bank for sight restoration. Upon her death in 1948 in the Methodist Hospital her eyes were flown to Baltimore where the corneas were transplanted. Today someone else is seeing through the eyes of Harriett Hubbard. This is a parable of something more wonderful even than new corneas in the eyes of our bodies: to see the world with the eyes of Christ, the eyes of our hearts and minds made new. Millions of folk have done that. Think of the pages and pages that have been added to the gospel on account of what men have done seeing life with the eyes of Christ.

The vast social effort to make this a more decent world in which to live has come directly from what God declared through His prophets and His Son: that mankind are the children of God. The unimaginable struggles and towering crosses men have endured to achieve understanding between the races—none of this would ever have been thought of, let alone attempted, except for God's compassion as it shone in prophets and in Christ. Looking at the world through the eyes of Christ people have seen that there is something wrong with a world that produces extreme poverty in the midst of great wealth, that excludes some of the fairest sons and daughters of the earth because their skin is colored, that forces girls into prostitution to earn enough to live, that breeds such ugliness and frustration in its communities that men and women are driven to alcohol to escape defeats they cannot face.

But you see our concern for these things goes straight back to the Crucifixion and the Resurrection. It was because Jesus Christ rose from the dead that all human life is endowed with divinity. Men imagined it before him, but with his report they became sure. Because of the *eternal* possibilities and worth in men that Jesus disclosed to us, we are concerned with economic and social systems and what they do to people.

Shortly before he was killed in an air raid in London Lord Josiah Stamp, one of the great financial authorities of the twentieth century, gave an address over the B.B.C. dealing with standards of money. He ended his remarks by saying: "Before I finish I should like to say one thing, and it is this— I have not the smallest interest in what I have been talking about tonight, not the slightest interest in this or any other scale of values, except it accord with that other scale of values introduced into this planet by Jesus of Nazareth. This is the one and only scale of values that really matters, and which no man listening to my voice can ever afford to ignore, in peril of his soul." This from a man of money, accustomed to dealing with the financial fortunes of the world. You see, it is because men were made for eternity that they have such worth and inspire such sacrifice here. It was William E. Hocking who put it this way: "Draw your line around man at his death, cut across all lines of his aspirations, snuff out all his major questions, quash all his claims, declare all his unfinishedness a zero to the cosmos, and the nerve of all his concern for justice is also cut. Without his continuance his present cannot hold its own meaning and worth." You may say that this is beginning at the wrong end of affairs; that we have no right to postulate a future merely to buttress up a present in which much deserves to die. Hocking did not mean that, nor do we. It must be pointed out, however, that where life is all present and no future, all two-dimensional and with no vertical dimension, the bottom soon falls out. This is not so much proof of a future life as it is judgment on this life. Great pages have been added to the gospel of life in this world by people who through the Resurrection were persuaded of an eternal life for all who loved God.

4. And then what of the pages added to the gospel because of the way Christ transfigured death? In the assurance of his Resurrection men and women ever since have been able to look into the face of death without fear, finding in death the doorway to a friendly home. We have said more of this in earlier places in this book, believing that faith in eternal life ought to lie close to the heart of the gospel, not tucked onto the end. Here we have only to say that the Christian faith concerning death is that it is a crossing to a home with God. Not the same to everyone, death must at least begin as the affair that we have made of life. But to those who greet it in faith, although sorrow, heartache, loneliness be death's companions, the awful despair is gone.

A Man Called Peter is the life of Peter Marshall written by his wife Catherine.[1] Peter Marshall was the minister of the New York Avenue Presbyterian Church in Washington and chaplain to the United States Senate. In the last chapter of that book Catherine Marshall describes the night on which Peter was taken with his last illness. When a heart attack seized him an ambulance was called to remove him to a hospital. As he was being carried out the front door on the stretcher he looked up to Catherine's face and said, "Darling, I'll see you in the morning." She didn't know that night that those would be Peter's last words to her, nor in all likelihood did Peter think of himself speaking of morning other than the next day in the hospital. But what he said, and especially as Catherine Marshall remembered it, rings in our hearts as one of the most radiant expressions of Christian faith ever spoken. Because of Christ who himself said the same words in the Upper Room, "I'll see you again," because of his Easter victory, you and I can say to those we love who pass on into the valley, "Darling, I'll see you in the morning."

5. I have but one further word: Beyond the last page of the morning newspaper Christ holds the power to conquer the kingdoms of the earth. This is the world's great hope, born with the dawn of the Resurrection day: The final outcome of our history is not in the hands of the warmakers, the imperialists, the communists, or the ruthless destroyers of men's souls. It belongs to God! Just as the Roman cross belonged to God! This does not mean that it is "no contest," with the outcome already assured. It is very much of a contest with chances of defeat for individual enterprise and even for whole civilizations not only possible but likely! What this faith does mean is that the principalities and powers have been overcome;

there has been let loose in the world a power to redeem the tragedies and defeats of history; and it has already been demonstrated that God is more than a match for Satan.

You and I will not see this final victory over darkness spelled out in terms of earthly establishments, for this triumph lies at the far end of history. But it does give both purpose and destiny to the present struggle, and it is certain that we can move closer in our earthly kingdoms to the heavenly Kingdom which is above this world. And though battles be lost and new crosses raised along the way, the final issue is never in doubt. As Hugh Price Hughes put it in one of his greatest sermons: "If ever you hear anybody saying that slavery is necessary, that ignorance is necessary, that war is necessary . . . you can shout: Thank God that's a lie. Jesus Christ shall bring it about that right shall utterly prevail. Satan shall fall and his fall shall be sudden as it shall be irreparable." This great assurance turns despair to hope, it gives us heart to suffer and struggle on, forasmuch as we know that our labor is not in vain in the Lord. On the Resurrection morn Jesus Christ wrote a new last page to the world's life:

And the kingdom of this world has become the Kingdom of our Lord and of His Christ. And He shall reign King of kings, and Lord of lords, forever and ever, Hallelujah! Amen.

Notes

I. *The Inescapable Presence of God*

1. Robert Frost, from "The Road Not Taken" in *Mountain Interval* by Robert Frost. (Copyright, 1916, 1921, by Henry Holt and Company, Inc. Copyright, 1944, by Robert Frost.) Used by permission of the publishers.
2. Francis Thompson, "The Hound of Heaven" from *The Selected Poems* by Francis Thompson (London: Jonathan Cape Limited). Reprinted by permission of the publishers and the Executors of the Estate of Francis Thompson.
3. John Short, *Triumph Believing* (New York: Charles Scribner's Sons, 1952).

II. *Because God Is Our Friend*

1. *Life*, Dec. 24, 1951.
2. Henry P. Van Dusen. Quoted in *The New York Times*, Dec. 17, 1951.
3. John Masefield, *The Coming of Christ* (New York: The Macmillan Company, 1928), pp. 14, 22. Reprinted by permission of the publishers.
4. Maxwell Anderson, *Joan of Lorraine* (Washington: Anderson House, 1946), Act II.

III. *A Person-to-Person Call to God*

1. Richard Llewellyn, *How Green Was My Valley* (New York: The Macmillan Co., 1940).
2. Leslie Weatherhead, *Psychology, Religion and Healing* (New York and Nashville: Abingdon Press, 1951), p. 238.
3. G. A. Studdert-Kennedy, in *The Best of Studdert-Kennedy* (New York: Harper & Brothers, 1948), p. 26.
4. Joseph Wood Krutch in *Literary History of the United States*, edited by Spiller, Thorp, Johnson, Canby (New York: The Macmillan Co., 1948), Vol. II, p. 1247.

IV. *No Fear of Tomorrow*

1. Basil King, *The Conquest of Fear* (New York: Doubleday & Co., 1921).
2. Jacques Maritain, *The Range of Reason* (New York: Charles Scribner's Sons, 1952), p. 202.
3. Sidnew Lanier, "The Marshes of Glynn" from *The Poems of Sidney Lanier* (New York: Charles Scribner's Sons, 1884), p. 14.
4. Alan Paton, *Cry, The Beloved Country* (New York: Charles Scribner's Sons, 1948), p. 268.

5. W. H. Auden, *The Age of Anxiety* (New York: Random House, 1947), pages 42, 44. Reprinted by permission of Random House, Inc.
6. Sidney Lanier, *op. cit.*, p. 14.
7. Rufus Jones, *Spiritual Energies in Daily Life* (New York: The Macmillan Co., 1922), p. 5.

V. *How Christ Intercedes for Us*

1. Leslie Weatherhead, *Psychology, Religion and Healing* (New York and Nashville: Abingdon Press, 1951), p. 342.
2. George Bernard Shaw, "St. Joan" in *Seven Plays by Bernard Shaw* (New York: Dodd, Mead and Co., 1951), p. 905.
3. Rufus Jones, *The Radiant Life* (New York: The Macmillan Co., 1944), pp. 36–38.
4. John Galsworthy, *Swan Song* (New York: Charles Scribner's Sons, 1928), p. 353.
5. William Temple, *The Faith and Modern Thought* (London: The Macmillan Co. Ltd., 1910), p. 135.
6. Walter Marshall Horton, *Our Eternal Contemporary* (New York: Harper & Brothers, 1942), p. 83.
7. John Masefield, "The Everlasting Mercy" from *The Poems of John Masefield* (New York: The Macmillan Co., 1923), p. 86. Reprinted by permission of The Macmillan Co.

VI. *When Love Has the Last Word*

1. Mark Twain, "A Medieval Romance" (chap. 5, "The Terrible Catastrophe") from *Sketches New and Old* (New York: Harper & Brothers, 1929).
2. Leo Tolstoy, "God Sees the Truth but Waits" from *Twenty-Three Tales* by Leo Tolstoy, translated by Louise and Aylmer Maude (New York: Oxford University Press, 1906).
3. *Time*, Dec. 29, 1952.
4. Eugene O'Neill, *Days without End* (New York: Random House, 1933), Act IV.
5. Harold Bosley, A *Firm Faith for Today* (New York: Harper & Brothers, 1950), p. 169.

VII. *The Clemencies of God*

1. Rollo May, in *The Saturday Review*, Aug. 15, 1953.
2. George Santayana, "With You a Part of Me" from *Poems* by George Santayana (New York: Charles Scribner's Sons, 1923), p. 61. Used by permission of the publishers, Charles Scribner's Sons.
3. Amos Wilder, "Thanksgiving" from *The Healing of the Waters* (New York: Harper & Brothers, 1943), p. 32. Reprinted by permission of Harper & Brothers.

4. The phrase is from a poem "A Special Place" by Dorothy Quick, quoted in *The Questing Spirit*, edited by Luccock and Brentano (New York: Coward-McCann, 1947).
5. Albert Camus, *The Plague* (New York: A. A. Knopf, 1948).
6. Elizabeth Barrett Browning, "Substitution" from *The Complete Poetical Works of Elizabeth Barrett Browning* (New York: Thomas Y. Crowell Co., 1887), p. 357.
7. Catherine Drinker Bowen, *Yankee from Olympus* (Boston: Little, Brown and Co., 1944), pp. 404–5.

VIII. *But If We Suffer with God*

1. Marie Killilea, *Karen* (New York: Prentice-Hall, 1952), p. 25.
2. Laurence Housman, "A Prayer for the Healing of the Wounds of Christ" from *The Collected Poems of Laurence Housman* (London: Jonathan Cape Limited). Reprinted by permission of Jonathan Cape Limited.
3. Anne Brontë, "Last Lines" from *The Complete Poems of Anne Brontë* (London: Hodder and Stoughton, 1920), p. 148.
4. Marie Killilea, *op. cit.*, p. 212.
5. Rufus Jones, *The Luminous Trail* (New York: The Macmillan Co., 1947), p. 165.

IX. *Love Stands Also at the Heart of Death*

1. David MacLennan, *No Coward Soul* (Toronto: Clarke Irwin and Co., 1948), p. 241.
2. Coventry Patmore, "The Toys" from *The Poems of Coventry Patmore* (New York: Oxford Press, 1949), p. 365.
3. John Masefield, "The Widow in the Bye Street" from *The Poems of John Masefield* (New York: The Macmillan Company, 1923), p. 204. Reprinted by permission of The Macmillan Co.
4. Dana Burnet, "The Question" in *Post Stories* (New York: Random House, 1946).
5. Ruppert Brooke, "Safety" from *The Collected Poems of Ruppert Brooke* (New York: Dodd, Mead and Company, Inc., 1915), p. 108. Reprinted by permission of Dodd, Mead and Company.
6. Thomas Wolfe, *You Can't Go Home Again* (New York: Harper & Brothers, 1940), p. 743.

X. *False Gods and the Devil to Pay*

1. *The New York Times*, Oct. 5, 1952.
2. Quoted in *Faith and Education* by George Buttrick (New York and Nashville: Abingdon Press, 1952), p. 103.

3. Sir Arnold Toynbee, *A Study of History*, One Volume Abridgment by D. C. Somervell (New York: Oxford Press, 1947), p. 207.
4. Lilith Lorraine, "When Planes Outsoar the Spirit" from *Let the Patterns Break* (Avalon Press). Reprinted by permission.
5. V. A. Demant, *Religion and the Decline of Capitalism* (New York: Charles Scribner's Sons, 1952), pp. 88–89.
6. Robert Raynolds, *The Sinner of Saint Ambrose* (New York: Bobbs-Merrill, 1952), pp. 413–14.

XI. *Good News for a Beat Generation*

1. Clellon Holmes, "This Is the Beat Generation," *The New York Times Magazine*, Nov. 16, 1952.
2. Murray G. Ross, *Religious Beliefs of Youth* (New York: Association Press, 1950).
3. T. S. Eliot, "The Hollow Men" from *The Complete Poems and Plays of T. S. Eliot* (New York: Harcourt, Brace and Company Inc., 1952), p. 56. Reprinted by permission of Harcourt, Brace and Company.
4. Catherine Drinker Bowen, *Yankee from Olympus* (Boston: Little, Brown and Co., 1944), p. 197.
5. Maxwell Anderson, *The Eve of St. Mark* (Washington: Anderson House, 1942), Act II, Scene V. Reprinted by permission of Anderson House.
6. William Shakespeare, *King Lear*, Act I, Sc. IV.
7. Franz Werfel, *The Forty Days of Musa Dagh* (New York: The Viking Press, 1934), p. 151.

XII. *Life in Three Dimensions*

1. Reinhold Niebuhr, "The Impact of Protestantism Today" in *The Atlantic Monthly*, Feb., 1948.
2. James Moffatt, *The Thrill of Tradition* (New York: The Macmillan Co., 1944), p. 149.

XIII. *A Sight to Make Hell Tremble*

1. C. S. Lewis, *The Screwtape Letters* (New York: The Macmillan Co., 1942), p. 15.
2. T. S. Eliot, "The Cocktail Party" from *The Complete Poems and Plays of T. S. Eliot* (New York: Harcourt, Brace and Company Inc., 1952), p. 342. Reprinted by permission of Harcourt, Brace and Company.
3. Maurice Herzog, *Annapurna* (New York: E. P. Dutton, 1953).
4. Ola Winslow, *Meetinghouse Hill* (New York: The Macmillan Co., 1952), p. 65.

XIV. *Found in the Stars*

1. Maxwell Anderson, *Lost in the Stars* (New York: William Sloane Associates; Washington: Anderson House, 1950). Reprinted by permission of Anderson House and William Sloane Associates, Inc.
2. *Ibid.*
3. *Ibid.*
4. Edwin Markham, "The Consecration of the Common Way." Reprinted by permission.
5. Howard Thurman, *Jesus and the Disinherited* (New York and Nashville: Abingdon Press, 1949), pp. 50–51.
6. T. S. Eliot, "The Journey of the Magi" from *The Complete Poems and Plays of T. S. Eliot* (New York: Harcourt, Brace and Company Inc., 1952), p. 68. Reprinted by permission of Harcourt, Brace and Company.
7. John Erskine, "Kings and Stars" from *Sonata and Other Poems* by John Erskine (Indianapolis: The Bobbs-Merrill Company, Inc.) Reprinted by permission of The Bobbs-Merrill Company.
8. G. K. Chesterton, "The House of Christmas" from *Collected Poems of G. K. Chesterton* (New York: Dodd, Mead and Company, Inc., 1932), p. 129. Reprinted by permission of Dodd, Mead and Company.

XV. *Beyond the Last Page*

1. Catherine Marshall, *A Man Called Peter* (New York: McGraw-Hill, 1951), p. 261.